To
Franca

Keep #Crushing it

Lisa Gold

CRUSHING
MEDIOCRITY
10 WAYS TO RISE ABOVE
THE STATUS QUO

CRUSHING MEDIOCRITY:
10 WAYS TO RISE ABOVE THE STATUS QUO

Published by Crushing It Academy, LLC,
160 Terminal Road, Georgetown, TX 78628

Printed in the United States of America

ISBN: 978-0-9789323-2-9

CRUSHING
MEDIOCRITY

10 WAYS TO RISE ABOVE
THE STATUS QUO

by René Banglesdorf
& Lisa Copeland

Acknowledgements

Sometimes it's not until a project is finished that you realize how much time and effort actually went into it—and from so many sources. To our families and friends who sacrificed time with us so that we could write this book, we offer our gratitude for your understanding and appreciation of our dreams. We could not have put the following chapters together without the perseverance of Ellie Scarborough Brett, who helped us clarify our own messages and find the voice we share. And we owe many thanks to those who helped with editing: Eli Gonzales, Kari, Amy, Janet, and Adrian. You all have helped us build a legacy we are so proud to be living. Thanks for believing in us!

Foreword

Do you want a life that is ordinary…
Or a life that is extraordinary?
Do you want a career that is boring…
Or a career that is exciting?
Do you want to raise children who are average…
Or children who are exceptional?
Do you want to just get by financially…
Or do you want financial freedom?

You are the CEO of your own life! You have the power to choose each and every day what kind of life you want to live, a life of simple existence…Or a life of significance.

In *Crushing Mediocrity*, Lisa and René reveal the roadmap for living an extraordinary life of significance by becoming a change agent for good.

We must be purposeful, we need to rely on and encourage one another, and we must be prepared to rise above the status quo every chance we get. Sometimes the chances we take work out. Sometimes they don't. But without taking chances on others, we cannot help them.

The mere phrase "taking chances" may invoke the fear of change in some. It means stepping out of your comfort zone. It means feeding your curiosity. As young children, we were curious about everything…some would say we were fearless. We learned by doing and experimenting. What changed as we grew older? We were taught conformity. One of the greatest problems with conformity is that it punishes…and eventually can kill our curiosity.

The most successful businesses today were started by entrepreneurs following their curiosity. In our everyday lives, curiosity is what triggers the desire for exploration, it helps us step out of our comfort zone, and it creates a love for lifelong learning.

Walt Disney said, "We keep moving forward, opening new doors, and doing new things, because we're curious and curiosity keeps leading us down new paths."

When was the last time you were curious? When was the last time you opened a new door?

By opening new doors, your curiosity will help you discover new opportunities. By pursuing those opportunities, you can turn them into possibilities and eventually, into realities...but it all begins with curiosity.

What holds us back from opening new doors? Mediocrity, complacency and sometimes busy-ness. I have had the honor of working with people striving for financial success for many years. Those who succeed learn how to break through their fears, embrace their curiosity and pursue lives of significance.

They learn to recognize when they have filled their lives with such busy-ness, that they have no bandwidth left to allow their curiosity to flourish. They learn that sometimes you need to close one door in your life in order to allow other doors of opportunity to open for you.

At the young age of 25, I discovered my own way to trigger my curiosity. I was in a successful career in public accounting at the time, yet felt there was more for me to do. I had received an offer from a client to join him in a new company. In analyzing the decision, I found myself listing the pros and cons of leaving my successful and "safe" career. And yet the list didn't help me at all... as I could still argue both sides of the decision. It was at that moment that my hand took over and wrote across the top of the page, "Why Not?" We are often told the importance of finding our "why" in determining our purpose and passion in life. But it is asking yourself "Why Not?" that will kick you into action, spur your curiosity, and provide you the courage to pursue it-- crushing mediocrity in your own life.

I still employ my "why not?" philosophy today as

a way to challenge myself to continue expanding my horizons and seizing new opportunities.

Our most precious resource in life is our time. Start by reviewing how you currently spend your time. Is it moving you forward, or holding you back? Is it feeding your curiosity, or stifling it? You may need to close a door or two on how you have been spending your time to break through the mediocrity you discover... in order to engage your curiosity. The opportunities and possibilities are limitless!

Lisa and René have discovered how to live extraordinary lives and have become exceptional change agents for good. In *Crushing Mediocrity* they invite you to join them by revealing their personal journeys and what they have learned along the way. You have an opportunity to accelerate your own journey. Will you take action? Will you allow your curiosity to guide you? Now ask yourself, "Why Not?"

To your success!

Sharon L. Lechter, CPA CGMA

Author of *Think and Grow Rich for Women*
Co-author of *Outwitting the Devil, Three Feet From Gold,* and *Rich Dad Poor Dad*

Table of Contents

Introduction.............................. 1

Identify Your Purpose........................ 7

Exit Your Comfort Zone.....................17

Own Your Choices...........................27

Remain Teachable...........................39

Operate Together...........................49

Stand Out....................................61

Repurpose Your Fears.......................71

Recover From Failure.......................83

Use Your Influence For Good...............95

Become a Change Agent...................109

Conclusion.................................121

Introduction

What do you want out of life?

Seriously, is your goal to finish in the middle of the pack, with a humdrum existence, unremarkable career, or average kids? We hope not. It doesn't benefit any of us. Yet many people today seem to be drifting in a river of mediocrity. Some may blame it on "the system," or lack of opportunities, or too low of a minimum wage. They may have experienced a troubled childhood, a missed promotion, or a divorce. But everyone has at least one thing in common: the option to rise above the status quo, to crush mediocrity, and to change the world around them.

The truth is, *You* have the option to do all of these things. You too can improve your world, rise above the status quo, and crush mediocrity. And you can make an impact right where you are today. Whether you are young or old, male or female, a teacher's aide or a senator, a mechanic or a CFO, a police woman or a stay-at-home-dad, you can leave a mark on your world. It will take determination and hard work, but you can do it. Even if it means adopting a new perspective or enduring a less-than-comfortable change, we know you can do it. We can all do it! Just imagine the possibilities if we all are brave enough to make that pledge and see it through.

Together we could improve our lives, our families, our communities, our schools, our churches, our penal system, our nation, our planet.

One of our friends has taken exactly that approach. Gigi Edwards Bryant grew up in the Texas foster care system five decades ago. She was separated from her three siblings, shuffled through more than 20 homes over the course of 12 years. And to make it even worse, she was sexually abused by several foster family members. With such a background, she was expected to fail by the very system that was created to protect her. Gigi had every reason to simply adopt a victim mentality and become a despondent statistic. However, she clung to her grandmother's teachings of faith and instead of becoming a sad statistic, she built a legacy.

Gigi chose a path that required everything she had and then some. Instead of the popular liberal arts route, Gigi studied computer science in college while caring for her family and holding down a full-time job, and not at the local burger joint either. She worked at several state agencies, including the Comptroller of Public Accounts, Parks and Wildlife, and the Texas Legislative Council. But even that wasn't enough for her. Gigi made it her life's goal to serve as an advocate for education and for the young people she now calls "our children" in the child protective services program.

She got involved in the community, something she never had the opportunity to do as she was shuffled from "home" to "home" and school to school while growing up. As an active volunteer, she eventually was appointed as chair of the Texas School Safety Center by Governor George W. Bush. She also was recognized by Governor Rick Perry when asked to be the head of the Texas Department of Family Protective Services Advisory Council—a place she knew she could make a difference because she had experienced the problems first-hand.

Gigi regularly shocks us with how wide and how far her reach extends in making an impact. Recently a group of us were enjoying a relaxing day at the spa (lounging around in nondescript white robes sans makeup), when Gigi said, "Oh, there's my friend Gayle King. We worked on some stuff together. Do you want to meet her?" Of course, we did. The CBS morning-show host and Oprah's best friend invited us to pull up chairs and hear how impactful our humble friend Gigi has been. We had no idea.

Today Gigi holds a board position at Austin Community College, which provides vocational training or continuing education for more than 50,000 students a year. She works relentlessly to help others rise above their circumstances, no matter their beginnings. She says she focuses her life's work around education and foster children because these institutions affected her life so greatly.

Gigi's mark on the world was born from a painful childhood, limited choices, and a determination not to settle for the status quo. Your mark on this world begins with who you are and accelerates with what you do with what you have. It's found in intentional daily living, with an end in mind.

As business leaders and authors, our lives also have been marked by daily decisions—the good choices as well as the bad ones. Through it all, we have found our own ways to move ahead, blazing a trail for our families, our careers and our communities.

We both found our opportunities to disrupt the status quo in good-ole-boy networks—automotive and aviation. While being women in male-dominated industries does present unique challenges, we've discovered some foundational truths that transcend gender, job fields, or responsibilities. These are common denominators in earning a good reputation, building healthy personal and professional relationships, and leaving an extraordinary legacy. We both follow practices that help us disrupt the status quo in our industries and challenge mediocrity in our spheres of influence. This is what we hope to impart to you.

Named as one of the most powerful women in automotive this decade by *Automotive News*, Lisa sits among the most elite businesspeople in the country as a revolutionary in her industry. As managing partner of the Austin Fiat dealership, Lisa helped launch the Fiat brand in the United States and held the spot as the number one dealership for four out of five years in that role. She served four terms on Fiat Chrysler Automobiles' National Dealer Council, won several national best workplace awards, and is an advocate for women in the automotive industry.

René owns and runs a private jet sales company, also in Austin. She and her husband started Charlie Bravo Aviation in 2008, just before the general aviation industry began the worst downward spiral since the Wright brothers started powered flight. By using the principles outlined in the following chapters, she has managed to build the company into one of the top aircraft brokerages in the world, and one of the few woman-led companies of its type. In a 96-percent male-led industry, René's aim has been to promote higher integrity in a vastly unregulated market and to encourage more women to consider aircraft ownership or careers in the aviation field.

While both of us have succeeded as women in fast-paced, male-dominated fields, our personalities are as different as can be. Lisa's bold, visionary, outgoing nature contrasts with René's analytical, more introverted personality. That's how we know these principles work universally. We each use them from completely different perspectives.

The two of us believe in standing our ground, performing at a high level, and maintaining a healthy quality of life against all odds. We don't subscribe to ideas like settling, good enough, and status quo, and neither of us encourages people who complain about the way things are but do nothing about it.

We still strive to do the things our parents taught us as children growing up on opposite sides of the country—putting our best foot forward, telling the truth, earning our way, and respecting those around us—but as we look around, those qualities don't seem to be valued anymore.

Communication by text messaging, online dating, always-on-24/7 jobs fueled by smartphone applications, and unprecedented access to information have disrupted the way we learned to relate as well as how we balance and enjoy success. Coming advances in artificial intelligence may help clear some of the clutter, but they also give us more excuses to drift or coast or settle. If that's not what we want, we must do something disruptive ourselves.

We're ready to work diligently and make some sacrifices for the sake of generations to come, and it's our sincere hope that if you are drawn to this book, you are too. Crushing mediocrity is a lifestyle we embrace from a shared belief that what we see evolving in today's society is not the legacy we want to leave. So together, we are raising a battle cry to transform the future into something we can all celebrate. We want to continue impacting our sphere of influence in a positive way, and we want to challenge you to do the same.

That is the impetus for this book. We decided to start the conversation about rising above our mistakes, short-comings, and epic failures. Even if just a small percentage of people join us in the challenge to crush mediocrity, we can change the world.

This movement starts with us, and it starts with you. We may not know your exact struggles or fears. We may not know the challenges that stand in your way, but we are intimately acquainted with ours. Some we still face every day. However, we persevere, recover, strategize, renegotiate, thicken our skin, and take more risks. When the odds are overwhelmingly against us, we don't run, quit, or shrug our shoulders and say, "Well, at least we got this far." No, we focus on the legacy we are determined to build, and we keep going. You can do the same.

When we all focus on rising above the status quo, we can turn complacency into life-saving innovations and global competitiveness. We can replace political correctness with authenticity, and come up with real solutions to social ills. We can stop "just minding our own business" and get involved in making a difference in the lives of others. Together, we can encourage and mentor a generation that's growing up on social media to make an unprecedented impact on the real world. They have short attention spans and lack long-term planning skills. They need our guidance. We *must* inspire, empower, encourage and motivate them.

We can't do any of this by pointing fingers, and we certainly can't do it alone. Our success depends on you joining the fight.

Be brave. Crush mediocrity. Take some risks. Redefine *your* legacy. The world is waiting for you to do something to change it. What are you waiting for?

1

Identify Your Purpose

*We believe your unique purpose helps you
rise above the status quo.*

Most toddlers have a favorite word: *why*. It signals a sense of wonderment and inquisitiveness. This curiosity makes three-year-olds both endearing and annoying.

As we age, our questions shift from "Why is the sky blue?" or "Why did that man say a bad word?" to the more complex: "Why do bad things happen to good people?" and "Why am I here?"

Our questions become driven less by an insatiable appetite to learn, and more from a lack of fulfillment in our lives. We believe there should be more to life.

Why is life so hard to figure out? Maybe it's because we haven't found our true purpose yet or maybe we're trying to be someone we are not.

According to the Association for Psychological Science, developing a sense of purpose may add years to your life. Patrick Hill of Carleton University in Canada and Nicholas Turiano of the University of Rochester Medical Center studied over 6,000 people and did a follow-up 14 years later.[1] They concluded those who reported a greater sense of purpose and direction in life were more likely to outlive their peers.

Lead researcher Patrick Hill said: "Our findings point to the fact that finding direction for life, and setting overarching goals for what you want to achieve can help you actually live longer, regardless of when you find your purpose. So the earlier someone comes to a direction for life, the earlier these protective effects may be able to occur."

Anthony Burro, a developmental psychologist at Cornell University, tested this theory. Not only did he concur, but he found that those who found a sense of purpose also protected themselves from much of the stress in their lives.[2]

We believe you are on this earth for a unique purpose; you are here to share your gifts, talents, skills, and life experiences. This purpose gets you out of bed in the morning and helps you continue in the face of adversity. It also awards you the greatest sense of accomplishment. You may not know what your purpose is or how to pursue it, but the world is missing out on something if you are unable or unwilling to discover or fulfill it.

Unless you are intentional about your purpose, you slide toward *living a life without purpose*. Try as you might, without purpose, you will feel aimless, chaotic, pointless, random, indecisive, fruitless, impotent, inconsequential, ineffective, and trivial. Who wants any of that?

When you are are not walking in all you could be, you can become mired in mediocrity.

As a couple of boot-wearing Texas women, we are committed to crushing that mediocre mindset. In this book, we share stories and practical applications we've learned. It's our hope to leave you with clear ideas for crushing mediocrity, first in your life, then in the lives of those you influence most, and finally in the world around you. We won't claim to have arrived, but we're willing to share our journey and labor with you along the way.

Find Your Underlying Purpose

We believe that to rise above the status quo, you need to know and operate in your underlying purpose. If you don't know why you are here—or you feel like your mission might need some refining—the next few pages should help. If you already know what your purpose is, use the following points and suggestions to help others find theirs.

We define our underlying purpose as our *why*. If you haven't seen Simon Sinek's Ted Talk[3] or read his book *Start with Why*,[4] we highly recommend them. Simon suggests that many people can tell you what they do and how they do it, but they fail to define why they're doing it. He gives examples of individuals and companies who can define what they do and how they do it, but by starting with the "why," they become radically different from their competitors.

An underlying purpose fuels you. It guides your career choices, your extracurricular activities and even the way your personality develops over time. Thinking about it keeps you up at night. Purpose drives you to keep going when your brain tells you to quit. It awakens you and inspires you.

Lisa's underlying purpose is to empower women. Outside of her family, everything she chooses to do stems from this passion. Lisa is known as an automotive sales expert. In fact, she owned one of the best car dealerships in the nation. But her purpose is not in breaking sales records. It's to help women feel valued in every aspect of life. It's hiring women and teaching them sales or management skills. It's chairing the American Heart Association initiative to educate women about the risks of heart disease. It's raising a half a million dollars to fund STEM (science, technology, engineering, and math) initiatives for Girl Scouts. It's helping other automotive leaders develop a culture that engages, encourages, and empowers women.

If you look at Lisa's social media outlets, you see all sorts of encouragement for women, from personal congratulations, to inspirational quotes, and even funny pictures. The causes and charities she supports primarily serve women. No doubt about it, Lisa's purpose is to empower women.

René's underlying purpose is coming up with creative solutions to problems. She feels most fulfilled when she negotiates a contract, helps someone navigate a difficult situation, figures out a clear and accurate way to tell a story, or equips others to make good decisions. She funds charities that help people help themselves, from the Feeding Cabo Kids fishing boat ministry to an anti-trafficking organization in Cambodia that rescues women and teaches them how to design and sew purses from reclaimed fabrics.

Her purpose is somewhat harder to peg than others because it operates under the surface in everything she does. But if you look closely, it's the common denominator to her passions, not the outward display.

It took time for us to figure out how to teach people how they can discover their purpose. After quite a bit of research and a few marathon dinner conversations, we decided there are many ways to go about the process. You might already have a good idea. Sometimes life circumstances change your purpose. At the end of the day, you must explore the possibilities. Here are some concepts that may help:

You Just Know

Lisa's purpose never really needed to be uncovered. In her words, "It's just who I am," and everyone else knows it too. For instance, a few years back she got a call from another car dealer who told her she just had to meet a young woman named Stacy Johnson. He said that Lisa would love her because she was a single mom trying to make a difference in the world.

Not only did Lisa meet Stacy, but she also ended up hiring her, even though she knew that Stacy would be there for only a short time. Stacy grew up in foster care, and she had a dream and a passion for opening a foster house that would make a difference to some hurting kids. Lisa opened her heart and her contact list and did everything possible to help Stacy. Sure enough, six months later, Lisa was there to celebrate the grand opening of Stacy's foster house.

The mutual friend who called knew Lisa well enough to know that she would want to invest in this young world-changer. And by operating in her underlying purpose, Lisa empowered someone else to crush mediocrity and fulfill her own underlying purpose.

You Build Upon a Crisis

René met Kisha Makerney when she guest-hosted a television show that honored wounded veterans with fun hunting trips. Kisha was in her early 20s and had a prosthetic leg. Her story is inspiring. She completed her first tour of duty in Iraq at age 19. When she came home, she took her motorcycle to a local store to rent a movie. After experiencing a front tire blow out, she lost control of the bike and hit a road sign. Her leg was severed in the crash. She was in a ditch, alone, her leg attached only by a piece of ligament.

Her first thought about her future was not that she wouldn't be able to wear high heels at her wedding, nor feel the sand with all ten toes. Kisha's first thought was that because she had only one leg, the Army would never let her go back to train soldiers in an oppressed part of the world. She had dreamed of serving her country her entire life, and now, just three short years into living her dream, it was threatened by a crisis.

Through a lot of hard work and a strong faith, Kisha became the first woman to return to a combat zone with a prosthetic limb when she was deployed to Iraq in 2008. Then, after she came back to the States from this second tour, she became a highly competitive sharpshooter. Mastering that, Kisha set out to accomplish another first. She earned a warrant officer slot with the Army's Rotary Wing Flight Program, which made her the first Army amputee with a prosthetic limb to challenge the Army's flight school.

Kisha has had to battle for good medical attention because her injury didn't occur in the line of duty. She worked through discrimination, an abusive relationship, and a prosthesis so ill-fitting she is often on crutches to continue living her purpose to protect our country. That's crushing mediocrity and building a legacy of hope for those who follow.

You Answer a Higher Calling

We would be remiss in not mentioning the most popular book of all time regarding purpose, Rick Warren's *Purpose-Driven Life*.[5] Rick starts his book with two quotes. The first from atheist Bertrand Russell: "Unless you assume a God, the question of life's purpose is meaningless." The second quote is Colossians 1:16 from the Message translation of the Bible, "For everything, absolutely everything, above and below, visible and invisible, … everything got started in [God] and finds its purpose in him."

Rick goes on to say that our purpose is not about us: The purpose of your life is far greater than your own personal fulfillment, your peace of mind, or even your happiness. It's far greater than your family, your career, or even your wildest dreams and ambitions. If you want to know why you were placed on this planet, you must begin with God. You were born by his purpose and for his purpose.

The search for the purpose of life has puzzled people for thousands of years. That's because we typically begin at the wrong starting point – ourselves. We ask self-centered questions like what do *I* want to be? What should *I* do with *my* life? What are *my* goals, *my* ambitions, *my* dreams for *my* future? But focusing on ourselves will never reveal our life's purpose.

No one epitomizes this better than our friend Lori Champion. Lori, her mom, and her two younger brothers always sat in the front row at her dad's church in New Orleans. One particular Sunday, when the car was packed to leave for spring break right after service, Lori's life changed forever. In the middle of the sermon, her father had a heart attack and fell dead at the pulpit.

After that loss, Lori went to Louisiana State University to study advertising because she was determined not to follow in her family's footsteps to go into the ministry. She felt she had sacrificed enough. But she eventually realized that she couldn't escape her calling. Lori feels her underlying purpose is to connect people to their destiny. She does that today as a senior pastor at a large church in Austin, as the head of women's ministries for the Association of Related Churches, as an advisor for Women of Faith, and as someone who doesn't forget anyone.

Lori can remember details from conversations years earlier that help her connect people who she believes might work well together or bond over a common experience. With thousands of church members, it's remarkable that she knows so many people by name, but she claims this kind of gift is what happens when you're living your God-given purpose. Hers is to connect people to their destiny.

You Do Some Soul Searching

You may feel that you're not that passionate about any one thing and that if you could just stir up some strong emotions about anything, maybe it would inspire you to do something significant. René's search for her purpose took this path.

After a milestone birthday, she began questioning herself about what she was doing with her life and how she wanted to be remembered at the end of it. Her questions remained unanswered. Meanwhile, to come up with fresh marketing messaging for her company, she signed up for a Media Bombshell seminar, which turned into something different than what she expected.

In a small group setting of all women, the leader, Ellie Brett, asked each woman to identify her character strengths. Then she asked them what characteristics they saw in each person in the group, people they had only met that morning. The results were surprising. Each woman learned something new about herself that day. Ellie then told the participants to go home and ask those closest to them what they observed. René complied.

She was told she was confident, detail-oriented, honest, discerning, a good manager, and diplomatic. Her husband said she was a problem solver. Her daughter-in-law told her that she didn't let conflict simmer: she got it on the table at the first opportunity and dealt with it.

René reflected on her strengths along with the things she enjoyed in life and work—performing to the best of her ability, having harmony, making others better by being around her, and learning new things.

Then she looked for a common denominator. She likes puzzles. She majored in journalism to investigate stories. She loves her job when there's a fresh challenge. And voila, the purpose revealed itself, like a gold nugget in a pan of silt and rock. René's underlying purpose is to get to the bottom of things and solve problems in a way that others might not have considered. She likes the combination of creativity and analysis.

If you haven't identified your purpose yet—or if you're living it and trying to help others find one—you are reading the right book. We've identified four different ways you can find your purpose. However, having an idea of what your purpose might be without acting on it won't do you any good. We challenge you to find your purpose and exercise the fortitude to fulfill it. For either task, here's where you can start.

First, think about your character strengths. Write them down. Don't do it later, do it now. Grab a pen and paper or write in this book (okay, take notes electronically if you are reading an e-book.) Go ahead. Get the pen!

Now, list your character strengths. Be honest with yourself.

Second, ask others what they see in you. You might not be able to do that this very moment but make a point of doing it soon, while your curiosity is fresh. For now, work with your list of your character strengths.

Third, identify the things you love to do. Then analyze what it is you love about them.

Fourth, examine the lists, the list of your strengths and the list of things you're passionate about. We can't tell you exactly when it will happen, but it's right about this point when an underlying theme starts to make itself known. If not, you may have to dig deeper.

As an example, we can look at René's son Jake who is passionate about college football. It connects him with people. He played football. He can talk about football intelligently. He can share an afternoon building a friendship with someone while watching a football game. It's all about relationships for him. Football is merely a conduit that allows him to foster friendships and professional relationships. His underlying purpose is to build relationships.

Identifying your underlying purpose may require some soul searching and some analytical thinking. But once you figure out what awakens you, what keeps you going, at what part of the day you get your second wind, and what makes you pump your fist in the air, your purpose will become clear to you, which is a fist-pumping occasion if there ever was one.

Now, begin making choices based on purpose. Those choices will help you build a legacy that changes the world.

2
Exit Your Comfort Zone

You cannot crush mediocrity without taking risks.

Nothing was easy for American troops as they made the amphibious trek from the ocean to the beach. Nothing was given to them. The date was June 6, 1944. The fate of the world hung in the balance.

One soldier who was there told us, "There is nothing comfortable about standing in the ocean, keeping your shoulders just below the waterline, surrounded by the bloody carcasses of your best friends, trying not to be the next casualty of Normandy." The shores were soaked with the blood of American soldiers, many who had willingly signed up to fight. It was the first time most of them had experienced battle, yet their courage held strong, a true testament to their character.

When discussing *character*, we feel it apropos to mention this generation of men and women who *willingly* sacrificed a comfortable life for the greater good of generations to come. Our petty grudges and brief excursions from our comfort zones are embarrassing when held in the light of their sacrifice and commitment. From this era came the legacy that made Tom Brokaw dub them the

Greatest Generation. He said, "They came of age during the Great Depression and the Second World War and went on to build modern America -- men and women whose *everyday lives* of duty, honor, achievement, and courage gave us the world we have today."

The character you exhibit in your everyday life is the foundation of your legacy. The problem is many people don't know how to allow the right kind of character to develop. Let's first establish what character is. Dictionary. com defines character as "an aggregate of features and traits that form the individual nature of some person or thing."[6] CITRS, a non-profit, non-partisan, non-sectarian education company, describes character as a person's pattern of behavior, thoughts and feelings based on sound principles, moral judgments, integrity, and the "line you never cross."[7]

The problem today is that we don't live in an era where character is as important as it was just one generation ago. Today, people judge you by how much you make, your personal preferences, or what you do, and not by how you go about your daily life. In his book *The Road to Character*, David Brooks states, "We live in a society that encourages us to think about how to have a great career but leaves many of us inarticulate about how to cultivate the inner life."[8]

The book goes on to teach that people who focus on their careers or what others think of them find themselves doing things that other people approve of, whether these things are right for them or not. They foolishly judge other people by their abilities and never recognize their true worth. The problem is they don't have a strategy to build character, and without that, both their inner and external lives will eventually fall to pieces.

It's up to you to decide whether, through the actions you take in your everyday life, you build a character of excellence or a completely unremarkable testament to mediocrity. Here are some strategies you can use to build character:

Make Sacrifices

In our era of instant gratification and on-demand delivery, we have limited experience with not being able to buy what we want. We cannot imagine the government telling us what to buy or not buy—especially the basic necessities of life. But in the 1940s, wartime changed the consumer landscape of America. Things we take for granted were in short supply due to limited imports. For instance, the Japanese takeover of plantations that produced 90 percent of America's rubber limited the availability of tires, garden hoses, and raincoats.

War efforts also changed the demand for raw materials. Aircraft manufacturing in the 1940s increased exponentially. Approximately 2,000 planes were manufactured in the U.S. in 1939. An estimated 300,000 were made between 1940 and the end of the war. Aircraft manufacturing became the number one industry in the U.S. during World War II. This dramatically increased the need for steel and other components.

Nylon was used for parachutes and women had to do without stockings. While today that's a sacrifice many women wouldn't be that upset about, back then women primarily wore dresses and skirts with nylon stockings and heels. To remain fashionable, they improvised by drawing lines on the backs of their legs to have the appearance of a stocking seam.

Farmers and producers of consumer goods worked in factories or became soldiers. The limited workforce—and more women working in factories to support war efforts—caused a food production slowdown, and a global food shortage resulted. The Office of Price Administration issued ration books that specified the food each man, woman, and child was allowed to buy.

Quite the opposite of food stamps today, the ration books gave Americans access to pay for such everyday items as sugar, flour, meat, cheese, coffee, shoes, tires, and gasoline. Major purchases such as automobiles, bicycles, and kitchen appliances required special certificates and proof of need. Because the military needed typewriters for communication, even they were rationed. The first ration books were issued in the spring of 1942, and most rationing did not end until 1945.

When we talk with our elderly female friends who lived through the time of limited sugar and meat and only four gallons of gasoline a week, they humbly say it was nothing compared to the sacrifices the men were making on both the Pacific and European fronts. They learned how to survive in lean times and were appreciative of what they did have.

The world we live in today is vastly different. Most of us do not have to ration basic commodities, but we are still faced with self-indulgent or sacrificial decisions in our everyday lives. Even in this over-indulgent time "having it all" is still a myth perpetuated by magazine covers and advertisers.

When their kids were small, Lisa and her husband James both worked in the automotive business. They had a nanny for Allix and JT. Because

> **"You can't have it all, but you can have what matters most."**
> –Lisa Copeland

the dealerships were closed on Thanksgiving, they happened to be home when JT, then three-years-old, choked and almost died. It served as a wake-up call for Lisa. She decided that the career sacrifice she would make if she stayed home to take care of her kids was not as big a sacrifice as the one she was making by not having as much time with them as possible.

Lisa and James decided to sacrifice her six-figure contribution to the family income so she could be more involved in their children's development. At that point in their lives, it meant more for Lisa to be home and have the time to build her children's character intentionally. Now that Allix and JT are grown and have families and careers of their own, Lisa's focus is back on her automotive career. She believes her sacrifices made her all the more successful when she returned to the industry 15 years after she left it.

Develop Drive

In an aviation career, with an office at a municipal airport, René meets all sorts of interesting aviators. One of the most fascinating is Congressional Medal of Honor recipient and retired Air Force Lt. Col. Richard "Dick" Cole. Born in 1915, Dick is one of the last living Doolittle Raiders. The Doolittle Raiders were 80 men from different backgrounds who undertook a dangerous one-way mission: fly over Japan, drop bombs, and land in a part of China that was still free.

They accomplished their mission and proved to the Japanese High Command that their home islands were not invulnerable to American aerial attacks. This forced the Japanese to shift from an offensive focus to one of both attack and defense. Within two months, the division of resources weakened the Japanese military enough that the tide of the war in the Pacific Theater changed.

What René found most impressive about Dick is not that he was part of a risky mission to improve public opinion and troop morale in the Pacific on April 18, 1942. His major contribution to society has been how he's lived the 70 years since the war's end. Dick remained an Air Force pilot, flying more than 30 types of planes over his 27-year service career.

On one particular test flight, a charming stowaway surprised him when she popped her head into the cockpit. Dick recognized her as a flying student who had ridden up on her bicycle earlier and asked if she could fly with them. Dick told her no because there weren't enough parachutes, which was the same reason he was forced to abort the flight and land the plane. On the ground, his co-pilot asked the young woman to write her phone number in a matchbook. She complied and then passed the matchbook to Dick with a smile. Married two weeks later, Dick and Martha were together for more than 60 years before she died of Parkinson's disease in 2003. She and the children they had together provided the impetus for his drive.

Dick still gets up every morning, makes breakfast, does farm chores, checks his pedometer to make sure he's walked a mile every day and speaks to anyone who will listen to his sage advice. He's motivated to keep himself active so he's not a burden on anyone and so he can continue contributing to his community.

His words of wisdom to the generations behind him are: Don't complain. Keep learning. Meet new people. Be an asset to society.

Dick is driven to live a life of excellence and leave an exemplary legacy. He understands that the opposite of *drive* is *entitlement*.

Know That You Are Not Entitled

Feelings of entitlement are the result of the misguided mentality of taking rather than giving, draining rather than contributing, taxing rather than investing. Our research shows varying numbers for Americans subsisting on government assistance. On the conservative end, 35 percent of Americans were receiving welfare in some form as of 2012. No economic models show how this—a large percentage of the adult population not earning a living or contributing to society—can be a sustainable plan for economic growth and development

Much deeper than the actual economic impact is the psychological one. Cultures that perpetuate a "gimme" mentality are self-destructive. Millions of parents teach their children that it's okay not to be productive, that just because you breathe within these shores, someone else will provide for you, even though you are more than capable of fending for yourself. This sense of entitlement is undermining the very fabric upon which this country was built.

Decades ago, long before this sense of entitlement grew to the magnitude it is today, President John F. Kennedy addressed it. He recognized this dilemma in one of his most famous quotes, "Ask not what your country can do for you, but what you can do for your country." In a world where we want a growing, more meaningful existence, we must take it a step further and ask ourselves not what our community or fellow man can do for us, but what we can do for them.

You are not "owed" a legacy. You must build one.

Maintain a Forward-Thinking Perspective

The men and women of the Greatest Generation were determined to leave a better America for their children. They remembered the Great Depression and planned for the future. Not only did they keep their eye on the ball, so to speak, but they remembered the goal was to win the game. They kept this perspective alive in the next generations of soldiers.

Lisa has employed several veterans at her car dealership, and one who stands out is Staff Sergeant Matt Bliss, who served six years of active duty and two years in the Reserves. After he'd worked in the Fiat service department for four months, Matt approached Lisa to ask if she would give him a chance in sales. He had no sales experience and no formal sales training. In the first month, Matt had double-digit sales. The second month, he broke a single-month sales record. The amazing part is that he did this in an organization that was breaking national sales records of its own.

When Lisa asked him the secret of his success, he attributed it to hard work and perspective. When it was 100 plus degrees outside, and other sales reps were enjoying the air conditioning inside, Matt was in the parking lot waiting for potential clients.

"It's not that hot," he told her. "Afghanistan was hot. And there were no commission checks there. That was for my country. This is for my family. They are both more important than my comfort." Matt Bliss is building a legacy. He's working with the end in mind and growing as a business person and a leader.

Perspective is a great motivator for personal growth. If you don't have an idea of where you are going, you will drift in mediocrity. Take some time to write down what's most important and post it in a prominent place.

Pursue Excellence, Not Perfection

Excellence is one of those words we often ignore in everyday language, as we often ignore the pursuit of excellence in our everyday lives. More often, people tend to seek perfection, but the problem with perfection is its unsustainability. The perfect child has a bad day. The perfect job goes awry at some point. The perfect community elects new leaders. The quest for perfection always disappoints.

Part of the reason perfection is so hard to obtain or maintain is that the millions of people that make up society each have a say in defining what it means. Excellence, on the other hand, comes from within; it's interpreted individually. Excellence happens when you do your best, and you know when you're there without needing approval from anyone else.

Striving for excellence throughout her life, former U.S. Ambassador to Finland Barbara Barrett has held leadership roles too numerous to count. Her story is one of sacrifice, strategy, achievement, and servant leadership. It started in earnest when she was 13 and her father died. Her mother didn't handle the loss well, and as the oldest, Barbara became the sole source of income for her household of six siblings and her mother. Barbara managed the family farm and charged people to ride her horses.

Compound those responsibilities with the fact that Barbara wasn't old enough to have a driver's license. Obtaining feed for the horses and supplies for her family was a constant struggle, but she persevered. Then when she went to college, she held down five part-time jobs to pay tuition and keep food on her family's table. Those years taught her the time-management skills that enabled her to be a partner in a large law firm in Phoenix and before she was 30, an executive in two global Fortune 500 companies.

Since then, Barbara has served on numerous corporate boards, has been the deputy administrator of the Federal Aviation Administration and was the U.S. Ambassador to Finland. She also has served as interim president of the Thunderbird School of Global Management, and with her husband, owns Triple Creek Ranch in Montana, named by Travel + Leisure as the best hotel in the world in 2014.

Barbara still challenges herself—and not with simple things, like learning to knit, either. Barbara has landed an F-18 Hornet on an aircraft carrier, climbed Mt. Kilimanjaro, driven cattle on horseback, and biked more than 900 kilometers in nine months in Finland. She even trained as an astronaut in her late 50s. Although Barbara exudes excellence, she continuously pursues it.

A refusal to compromise on excellence and integrity builds character and creates a foundation for success that stands the test of time, economic and emotional hardships, and unforeseen circumstances. It elevates you above the status quo.

Helen Keller once said, "Character cannot be developed in ease and quiet. Only through experience of trial and suffering can the soul be strengthened, ambition inspired, and success achieved."

To develop your character, you must make hard decisions about what is most important to you, and then be certain that your actions and everyday choices build on those priorities. You must keep driving toward the goal line without giving up or making excuses. No one else controls your destiny. You must pursue excellence with both the foundation and the future in mind, regardless of the disruptions life throws in your way. That crushes mediocrity.

3
Own Your Choices

The sum of your decisions—good and bad—will keep you in mediocrity or help you crush it.

We've all had the "what in the world was I thinking" moment. Yet, some hasty decisions have turned into blessings, and we would choose the same thing again.

Many of us also live with regret, wishing we would have acted or reacted to something in a different manner. In those situations, remorse can confine our dreams and expectations like a prison wall. It can limit us from becoming more. Instead of a life filled with great breakthroughs and success after success, the consequences of our choices can pigeonhole us into just going through the motions, haunted by our pasts.

This mediocrity remains in the lingering effects of bad decisions, festers in self-depreciation or doubt, and it often results in toxic relationships. These choices, made long ago, still affect the trajectory of our lives today. They are pockets of infection, whether on the surface or deep within, that we have never treated.

As we were writing this book, we both attended Michael Hyatt's online class called "5 Days to Your

Best Year Ever."[9] Before he even got to the goal-setting exercises, Michael had us identify "limiting beliefs" and their coinciding "liberating truths." Then he walked us through some exercises designed to help us, as he put it, "complete the past." These included the principles of acknowledging what happened, learning from the experiences, and adjusting our behavior accordingly.

We spent **40 *percent*** of our time in the "Best Year Ever" curriculum on exercises designed to help us overcome the limitations placed on us by our past. It's a step you cannot overlook. Our character has the space it needs to grow when the past is not crowding our present and our future. More importantly, our contributions have room to expand and become more powerful when the remorse from bad or mediocre choices no longer holds us back.

"Letting go" is a major factor in satisfaction with life—more than wealth, health, family, or religion. Studies show that harboring bitterness or holding a grudge is linked to an assortment of health problems, including stress-related infirmities and even cancer. More than 40 million Americans have been diagnosed with anxiety disorders, most of which are intensified by the sufferer's response to stressors.

Every single one of us is shaped more by our choices, and our response to the choices made for us, than any outside force.

Your cumulative decisions—from minuscule to enormous—determine your impact on your family, your workplace, and your community. The good news is that you have the power to direct this legacy. Following are some of the ways you can be stifled by your choices and some of the ways you can use them to buoy your success.

Don't Let Past Choices Bite Your Future

Many of us have a checkered past, some with more checkers than others. Choices have a knack of following us even after we've turned things around and become successful. This happened to our friend Rebecca Contreras.

Rebecca was born to a poverty-stricken, drug-addicted Hispanic mother in the late 1960s. She's one of four children, none of whom knew their fathers. As a child, Rebecca grew up in poverty, neglected and abused, a product of the trials that often plague children of single parents ill-equipped to provide for them.

At 17, pregnant and struggling with her studies, Rebecca dropped out of high school and began working as a cocktail waitress, even though she was underage. Rebecca was on a clear path to becoming a sad statistic. In the delivery room, she passed her daughter Crystaline to her mom, who had become sober some eight years before.

After a year of drinking, experimenting with drugs, and living irresponsibly on her own, Rebecca attended a church service at the insistence of her mother who at that time was raising her nearly one-year-old grandchild. That night Rebecca had a life-changing encounter with God, flushed her drugs down the toilet, and made a firm commitment to get her life on track. At the age of 19, Rebecca began the journey that would turn her life around.

She took responsibility for Crystaline, got her GED, enrolled in the Texas Welfare-to-Work Program, and met a dynamic youth leader, to whom she has now been married for 27 years. Rebecca moved through the ranks at several state agencies, learning how to maneuver office politics and increasing job responsibilities with finesse. She received promotion after promotion and ended up working for Governor George W. Bush. "Bec," as he calls her, was still working with him when he was elected President. As a star employee, Rebecca was faced with a major choice: keep her family in Texas with the jobs they knew or move to Washington D.C. to start over.

After much deliberation and prayer, Rebecca and her husband sold their house and moved their family across the country to join President Bush. At his request, she was commissioned as a member of his White House staff in the position of Special Assistant to the President and Associate Director of Presidential Personnel. In this role, she oversaw the President's appointments to more than 1,200 part-time board and commission positions in the federal government.

Part of the onboarding process for this federal job was a detailed background investigation. At that time, the Secret Service uncovered all sorts of things about her past. It was information typically not found on White House resumes. Rebecca knew that the past she thought she had left far behind had caught up with her. With her heart in her stomach, she headed into the West Wing office of her boss. Before this, Rebecca had been very private about her past, not wanting her teenage history to cost her future opportunities. The choices before her were to deny the findings, downplay or discredit them, or to admit her mistakes and be held accountable for her actions.

She decided to tell her boss the whole story and to clarify some of the Secret Service's findings. Because of Rebecca's transparency and the trust she had earned, her boss went to bat for her. Her job was not compromised. If anything, she garnered more respect as a woman who faced tremendous odds as a child, overcame them, and moved forward as an adult. Rebecca is a great example of someone who took responsibility for her past and her choices, yet she did not let them define her as a person.

After completing her White House post, Rebecca was appointed to serve on the West Point Military Academy board and at the Department of U.S. Treasury in the role of Deputy Assistant Secretary and Chief Human Capital Officer. Part of her duties included overseeing corporate human resources for a workforce of approximately 128,000 employees.

Today she runs her own company, AvantGarde, and is *crushing it* as a federal contractor with expertise in organizational development, human capital, and technology. She serves on the board of the American Bible Society as chair of the Committee on Governance. She also empowers and equips underprivileged teens and inner-city families in Austin through LaunchPad, a non-profit she co-founded with her husband. Realizing that she could attain more from life, exercising the will to keep on her new course, and then being honest about her mistakes has paid off for Rebecca.

A high school dropout and teen mother doesn't end up working for the President of the United States, advising West Point Military Academy, and running a company without making good choices after owning her bad ones. Her legacy is proof of what we can do if we are willing to accept where we are—and have been—but not let that determine where we are headed.

When choices are made for you, don't let bitterness hold you captive.

"Bitterness is like a cancer. It eats upon the host."
-Maya Angelou

René's mother, Myra, together with an older and younger brother, had a childhood filled with mistreatment from their alcoholic father. The worst abuse was directed toward Myra, the only girl and a sweet, mild-tempered peacemaker. Myra was both saddened and relieved when her father left home when she was 17. Then she had the opportunity to start a new life when she moved eight hours away to attend nursing school. Instead of blaming people for the abuse she had endured, she chose a life filled with love, got married, and had her first daughter, René.

While Myra's mom could (and did) hold a grudge for decades, René doesn't remember Myra being resentful or bitter. Instead, Myra chose to forgive people. She forgave her father for every bad thing he did to her. She also forgave her mother for not intervening. Myra even forgave herself for the feelings of shame that come along with being a victim of abuse. And when René rebelled as a teenager, Myra was on the other end of the tunnel with open arms.

The ultimate test of her forgiveness came 24 years after Myra's family fell apart. She was asked if she would go to Spokane to take care of the father who had never apologized. He had suffered a series of strokes and would spend the rest of his life confined to a nursing home. René witnessed in amazement as Myra flew to Spokane twice a year for 16 years to take care of the man she always called Daddy, despite the abuse. By the time they were reunited, he could barely speak. He couldn't voice any regrets and Myra never knew if he felt any remorse. But because his daughter made the trip two times a year he died knowing he was forgiven for his actions. Her brothers never visited their dad.

Forgiveness is a very powerful thing. Lewis B. Smedes, a 20th-century author and a professor, said, "To forgive is to set a prisoner free and discover that the prisoner was you."[10] The model of forgiveness that Myra showed her children was one of freedom, the liberty to live her life unfettered by the choices others made for her. Myra never chose to be abused, but she took matters into her hands and chose to forgive.

To move forward emotionally and spiritually, which can result in financial progress as well, you must understand that what other people do is out of your control. What is in your control is how you are going to react, and if you will allow those people or situations to hold you back. The ability to forgive is essential for anyone who wants to live for the future and not stay mired in past circumstances.

Sometimes You Pay The Price for Others' Choices

We don't know of anyone who has heard of or met Mary Barra and doesn't admire her. Mary worked her way up through General Motors, through good times and bad. She took leadership roles and overcame prejudices in a tough male-dominated industry. We can attest to the fact that there are a lot splinters on the climb up the corporate ladder. However, many of her coworkers say Mary never complained and never asked for special treatment or concessions because she was a woman. She just focused on doing her job well and climbed the ranks in the company she loved.

Mary was named CEO of GM in December of 2013, which made news because, well anytime there's a new CEO at GM, it's a big deal. But more newsworthy was the fact that Mary was the first female ever appointed as head of a major automobile manufacturer. GM made the news again shortly after she took office when evidence came to light that faulty ignition switches in GM cars had caused a number of deaths, and the cars had yet to be recalled. Mary didn't know about the issues, but others in the company did. The cover-up triggered Congressional inquiries, National Highway Traffic Safety investigations, a corporate settlement litigated by federal prosecutors, and a severely damaged corporate reputation.

Throughout the ordeal, Mary was the epitome of grace under fire. While she didn't shift blame, she did fire a dozen executives and restructured how the company handled safety defects. Under her watch, the company recovered from the 30-million-vehicle recall, which cost GM billions of dollars and resulted in low national consumer trust in 2014. In 2015, she rolled out strategies that halted the company's decline and shortly after that the company started to grow again. This humble, no-nonsense leader has become an icon in Detroit and around the world.

Is Mary considered by **Fortune** as the most powerful woman in the U.S. and by **Forbes** magazine as the fifth most powerful woman in the world because she sits in GM's CEO office and serves as Chairman of the Board? We don't think so. Mary is an amazingly powerful woman because she made hard decisions, she crushed the shady status quo, and she made it a priority to clean up an industry she had not sullied. That's the kind of legacy we should all want to leave.

Circumstances Can Derail You Temporarily—Don't Let It Become Permanent

In 1991, René was a typical overachieving college student. She was making good grades in one of the best journalism schools in the nation and juggling several leadership roles: a resident assistant in an upper-class dorm, senior writer for the school newspaper, and vice president of her sorority. She dreamed of graduating from Ohio University and becoming a top-notch investigative reporter.

On a cloudy day at the beginning of April 1991, the future she envisioned for herself was derailed. René walked from her dorm to the local CVS drugstore, checked to see if anyone there knew her, and bought a home pregnancy test. She then walked across the alley to a Wendy's, locked herself in a bathroom stall, and anxiously waited to see if a little pink line would predict her future. With a positive result, she realized the goals she had set for herself were no longer realistic. She got engaged that day and before the end of the year was a college dropout, a young wife, and a first-time mother.

However, she was still the same person who strived for excellence and who didn't let her unplanned circumstances change her. Instead of building a legacy as a world-class journalist, she focused on being a great wife and mother. The responsibilities of being a homemaker and the lack of a degree made it difficult for her to find work as a freelancer in suburban Washington D.C., where she and her husband Curt had moved for his job. But it was during those years when her priorities factored into her everyday choices that she gained the life skills that have put her where she is today.

She learned to be excellent in small everyday things, like making sure her children understood their home-work and keeping her house organized and clean in the midst of disappearing socks and other forms of chaos. She began to challenge herself to grow and learn new things on her own. Balancing a home, family, kids' sports schedules and a husband who traveled at the drop of a hat taught her time-management and quick-adjustment skills.

Today, her college journalism training helps the CEO of Charlie Bravo Aviation write clear contracts. Becoming an expert in communicating with her children and other parents has allowed her to flush out motives from difficult clients during negotiations and to communicate effectively with people from different socio-economic and cultural backgrounds.

When circumstances derail your plans, you can choose to feel sorry for yourself or make the best of it, pick a new path, and find an alternate form of success. When you feel you're not sure what do next, you might be exactly where you're supposed to be.

Allow Boundaries to Set You Free

Why does our society have such an aversion to the word *no*? Some parenting books actually discourage its use. Psychology pundits advise on redirection rather than refusal. But we lose something with all of this so-called positive reinforcement. We lose the ability to tell others and even ourselves *no*.

Consider the relative ineffectiveness of the "just say no to drugs" campaign. The campaign, in and of itself, wasn't a bad idea, but it was geared toward a nation with a disconnect to the word *no*. This is a systemic problem that perpetuates more negativity than positivity. We need to "just say no" to a lot more than drugs. Self-indulgence is crippling us.

Look at the increased consumer debt. Consider the number of unwanted pregnancies and extramarital affairs. Twenty billion dollars a year is spent on dieting in the U.S., yet 75 percent of Americans are still overweight or obese. I want you to read that again and let it sink in. We spend $20,000,000,000 a year on dieting in the U.S., yet 75 percent of Americans are still overweight or obese!

Many of us schedule every waking minute of every day. We're putting three-year-olds in dance classes and on soccer fields. We fit in friends and charity events and volunteering and yoga. We fool ourselves into believing we are building strong relationships, yet our smartphones are always present at the dinner table.

If you are going to leave an extraordinary legacy, you need to learn how to use the word *no*. You have to face the fact that you can't have it all, especially not all at once. You have to prioritize and establish boundaries. It's time to embrace the power in *not today* and *no thank you*. What we say no to defines our legacy every bit as much as what earns our *yes*.

Say *no* to things that don't match your goals. Say *no* to friends who are more interested in what you can do for them than they are in your company. Say *no* to time-eating events that take you away from the people you love and your plans. Say *no* to staying up late instead of getting up early. Say *no* to allowing yourself to believe your excuses. Say *no* to being dishonest. Say *no* to shifting the blame when it's yours. Say *no* to good enough. Trust us when we tell you it will do you good. When you say *no* to enough things that hold you back, you'll have more room to say *yes* to the activities that will lift you from mediocrity.

To re-define your legacy, you may need to kick the skeletons out of your closet, forgive yourself and others, fix problems you didn't create, make the decision to walk a new path, and set some boundaries. These are not tasks for the faint of heart. But then again, the faint of heart don't typically change the world.

4
Remain Teachable

*We believe in order to restore order to the chaos
that causes mediocrity, we must build respect.*

The San Antonio Spurs' black, white, and silver colors seem a perfect fit for a team whose persona is straightforward. The Spurs consistently provide a clear study in fundamental basketball with quick passes, well-executed plays, and precise shooting. The team's five NBA Championships have come under the leadership of head coach Gregg "Pop" Popovich. In 1997 he chose 6'11" forward Tim Duncan with the number one pick in that year's draft, spurring them on to a legacy of winning. The combo was a no-nonsense-yet-caring coach and a superstar who allowed himself to be coached and who never needed preferential treatment.

Tim's quiet demeanor and humble attitude made him an MVP on and off the court for his 19-year tenure on the Spurs. As a result, the culture of the team has become one of unselfish play and a family atmosphere. These talents, combined with team-oriented humility from the top of the organization to the bottom, provide the foundation for a franchise that has a higher and longer winning percentage than any other major league sports team in the U.S.

René is lucky enough to have the "Jack Nicholson" seats at the games of the Austin Spurs, the NBA Developmental League franchise owned by the San Antonio Spurs. She is a big basketball fan and loves her view from the floor, between the scorer's table and the visiting bench. She sits close enough to read the tattoos on the players' legs, arms, and shoulders and can hear the players on the court, which makes the game that much more exciting. However, some of the most interesting moments are spent watching the visiting coach and players interact. She has studied almost every coaching style in the NBA's D-League.

She has witnessed coaches get red-faced when yelling at their players and staff. She has seen coaches show up in wrinkled suits they probably wore as pajamas the night before and who barely communicate with their teams. She's also watched very instructional coaches who stay engaged the entire game. While players relate differently to these various coaching styles, René has noticed that for the most part players perform better for coaches who obviously care.

It is not uncommon to see San Antonio Spurs General Manager R.C. Buford make the trip to attend the games in Austin. Like head coach Pop, R.C. takes the composition of the staff and team seriously, even at the developmental level. Stories of team dinners and Pop and R.C. as father figures abound; and the family values are evident on and off the court. Players are recruited for their ability to fit in with the team, just as much as for their talent. And even though each of them brings a different skill set, the Spurs' persona doesn't seem to change. Two common denominators describe the Spurs: they are coachable and respectful.

From Pop on down, correction and instruction is well received by every single person affiliated with the Spurs. Those that give it are comfortable giving it and do it respectfully, a leadership trait not many possess. Those that receive correction don't take it as a personal attack because they know it's meant to make them better. It works.

It does little good to have the most talented players in the world if they roll their eyes at every suggestion or refuse to accept criticism or instruction and don't play well together. In sports, this leads to drama and a less cohesive unit. But the value of coachability transcends sports. A hard-headed mentality can poison an entire business or nonprofit environment.

Like any leader, you set the tone. Through a consistent and caring approach, you can have the same environment in your family, workplace, and community. But first, you must put authority in its proper place.

Acknowledge Authority

Part of being humble and growing is having a healthy regard for the proper order of things. A gross lack of respect for authority has fueled mediocrity and worse in our schools, workplaces, and communities. The antithesis of authority is anarchy, the breeding ground for terrorism.

There is no doubt about it, bullying is terrorism. Just ask one of the millions of teens who contemplate suicide each year. The U.S. Center for Disease Control and Prevention reports that 16 percent of high school teens have seriously considered suicide. As a result, more than 4,600 young lives are lost each year. Bullying is a leading cause.

The truth is that as a society we have become hypersensitive to hurting people's feelings. In our schools, parents have complained and complained so much about the way teachers have punished their children—most likely for good reasons—that it has restricted the schools' authority to discipline their students. The lack of authority has allowed the "bad apples" to go unchecked and now bullying is out of control.

Many take issue with teachers for reprimanding their children when they should be siding with their teachers and also reprimanding their children when they deserve it. Yet we make excuses for bad behavior instead of punishing it, and we enable it to worsen. Wouldn't we be better off picking suspension or appropriate punishments for bad behavior over rampant bullying?

In our workplaces, a lack of respect has reduced production and profitability. Many employees don't think twice about shopping online, surfing Facebook, or sending personal emails even though they are being paid to be there to work. They steal time they should be spending on company business for activities that do not benefit the company.

Showing up to work late, taking long lunches, and gossiping at the water cooler also show disregard for the urgency of company business. These behaviors, while they don't seem terrible, erode the foundation of a competitive advantage, putting companies unnecessarily at risk. It gets worse; some people disregard authority to the extent that embezzlement, fraud, and other criminal activities germinate.

Recent headlines highlight the lack of respect for authority in our communities. At times our police officers must defend themselves against armed criminals, and we see looting, vandalizing, and people obstructing justice. We also see people dying in our streets and in social settings. Racial tensions and hatred are escalating. We've all seen news footage showing blatant and mass disregard for law and authority. In these instances, we look more like a third-world country than the United

States of America that our veterans fought and died to protect.

If you want to crush mediocrity at every level, you must establish and model respect, which starts with honoring authority. Every action counts, whether it's an unseen act or someone yelling into a megaphone. This means you need to bite your tongue when you want to gossip about your boss with a co-worker, and you might have to show respect to your spouse even when you don't feel it. It may mean waiting until after a meeting to disagree with something someone said, so as to avoid undermining their authority.

René and her husband Curt struggled with this when they started Charlie Bravo Aviation. In the early years during team meetings, René contradicted Curt regularly. Sometimes he was wrong in what he said but more often, she just had a different opinion. The result was an entire staff that didn't respect either René or Curt as company leaders. Several employees took advantage of the situation and pitted the two against each other. The company became toxic.

René and Curt realized what was happening and became more of a united front as the leaders of the company. Even so, several employees kept exhibiting the old behavior. It wasn't until these people moved on that the company started to heal and gel.

Fostering a healthy respect for authority and other people creates environments with tremendous room for growth. These settings create champions and produce enviable legacies.

We'd be remiss in not giving a word of warning about those who abuse authority. Unscrupulous people can wield authority to belittle or use people instead of leading and protecting them. If you are in a position of authority, we hope you know that it's a privilege to guide and help others grow. The best leaders are great servants to those they lead. If you get to the point where you are considering something to be morally or legally wrong, use good judgment and stick to your core values. Whether we like it or not we are subject to a much higher authority, either the law of the land or God.

Never Stop Learning

It's not a good feeling to start a new job or role and feel as if we are in over our heads. We can be defensive, pretending like we know what we're doing, or we can take a realistic look at the situation and throw ourselves into on-the-job training. First-time parenting is a classic example. You're often sleep-deprived and probably dealing with crazy hormones, yet you're in a situation where the object of your responsibility cannot communicate with you except by crying. Smart moms quickly learn they need outside input.

A new job requires finding resources also. When Lisa left the car business to focus on her children, she was a mid-level manager. When she returned, she was a general manager. It was a bit like being thrown into a ring with boxing gloves on, staring at a trained fighter. Lisa decided that she must be willing to teach herself. The first couple of years, she spent her vacation time going to industry events where she could learn more about the issues she faced and how to keep larger issues from occurring.

Lisa read books. She found resources. She asked questions—inside her organization and out. She aligned herself with thought leaders in her industry, following them on Twitter, reading their blogs and engaging with their content. She listened and took notes. She enrolled in online courses for areas she needed to strengthen. And throughout this process she did what many others fail to do: she used the knowledge she gained. Lisa acted on the belief that the person responsible for her success was herself. Her drive showed that she was determined to succeed, but it was using her wisdom that transformed her into the leader she has become.

To expand your legacy, you must first acknowledge that you need to grow. To rise to the top, you must be willing to seek development opportunities. Your bosses or leaders or parents or team members are not necessarily going to push you to mature as much as you would push yourself. And frankly, it's not their responsibility. You're a grown-up. You get what you work for.

Recognize You Can Learn from Others

You should have the ability to receive feedback without being defensive. Great leaders are good listeners. Sometimes the best ideas come from the trenches—whether in a hostile, warlike situation or a collaborative brainstorming session. It pays to be willing to find better or easier ways to do things.

It also pays to have a good filter, to think for yourself, and to not be swayed by every argument. One way to become wiser is to be selective about who you listen to, and on which topics. It doesn't make sense to take career advice from a person who has never been promoted or marriage tips from someone who got married last week.

You need to be strategic in your mentoring relationships. Good mentors can be hard to find. We've all become accustomed to connecting, following, and friending on social media, but real life is different. It's inappropriate to walk up to any speaker at a conference and ask them to mentor us. That's just as awkward as a fifth-grade romance where the boy asks a girl to be his girlfriend, and once she shyly nods, he has no idea what to say next because they have nothing in common.

While finding the right mentor isn't easy, once you have, asking him or her to be your mentor can also be tricky. Facebook's COO Sheryl Sandberg compares the approach of some people seeking mentors to the little bird in the classic children's book by P.D. Eastman *Are You My Mother?*[11] The little bird asks a kitten, a hen, a dog, a plane, and finally a power shovel if they are his mother. In her own book, *Lean In*, Sheryl relates this to seeking a mentor. "This child's book poignantly mirrors the professional question 'Are you my mentor?' If someone has to ask the question, the answer is probably no. When someone finds the right mentor, it is obvious."[12]

In business, the most effective mentorships are often the most informal. Sheryl says:

"I have seen lower-level employees nimbly grab a moment after a meeting or in the hall to ask advice from a respected and busy senior person. The exchange is casual and quick. After taking that advice, the would-be mentee follows up to offer thanks and then uses that opportunity to ask for more guidance. Without even realizing it, the senior person becomes involved and invested in the junior person's career. The word *mentor* never needs to be uttered. The relationship is more important than the label."

René and Lisa have both had many people influence their careers, some completely without knowing they were doing it. It pays to be alert for opportunities to learn from people with different job responsibilities or even in other industries. As you seek help or advice, be respectful of their time. Sheryl advises:

"Few mentors have time for excessive hand-holding. Most are dealing with their own high-stress jobs. A mentee who is positive and prepared can be a bright spot in a day. For this same reason, mentees should avoid complaining excessively to a mentor. Using a mentor's time to validate feelings may help psychologically, but it's better to focus on specific problems with real solutions. Most people in the position to mentor are quite adept at problem solving. Give them a problem to solve. Sometimes high-potential [people] have a difficult time asking for help because they don't want to appear stumped. Being unsure how to proceed is the most natural feeling in the world. I feel that way all the time. Asking for input is not a sign of weakness but often the first step to finding a path forward."

Words of Warning

Be careful when you ask someone for advice. The worst thing you can do is ask for advice, not follow it, and then lose credibility with the person you asked for help, especially if they are in a position of authority in your organization or industry.

As you mature in life and your career, become a mentor. At this stage, the relationships from which you learn the most are more likely to be collaborative rather than mentor-like. Always be willing to give more than you receive; it pays off when you need it most.

5
Operate Together

We believe together we can accomplish
far more than we could alone.

Although we have been acquainted for more than a decade, our unlikely friendship blossomed several years ago when Lisa's business partner bought a Citation Jet. Lisa's newest obsession became having her own jet, and several cocktail parties and charity events later, we realized we had more in common than being women in a man's world.

Part of the reason we decided to co-author this book is because we share a frustration with the number of people we see stuck in the status quo. The truly infuriating part is they don't see it in themselves. They've found a level of contentment in their lives. It's as if their mindset is, "My bills are paid. That's all I need." It's sad to see people with so much potential fail to realize that they can achieve more. We've met people, both younger and older, who seemingly have given up on many facets of their lives— career development, great parenting, or pursuing their goals—and who have settled for where they've landed. It saddens us that they are okay with that. Part of the problem is they have surrounded themselves with people who have the same lack of drive and vision.

Change can be difficult, though, and it's more challenging to do things alone than with someone else. Dieting with a couple of friends is easier than dieting alone. Going to a spin class improves your likelihood of actually completing the workout and pushing yourself a little harder than you would if you did it at home. Riding a roller coaster is better with a friend to scream with; besides, she can hold your hair when you throw up afterward. These may be superficial examples, but the sentiment stands.

Our goal for this book is to challenge you to reach your full potential and share with you the changes that will empower your life, your career, and the community around you. We've talked in the last few chapters about how to crush mediocrity in your personal life. Now we shift the focus to include the world around you. Spoiler alert: It will still help *you*!

Find Others Going the Same Direction

We are big believers that change sometimes feels like the wind; it either gently pushes us along or opposes us like a mighty hurricane. Bob Seger's 1980 song "Against the Wind" is a great lyrical story about going eight miles a minute for months at a time, surrounded by strangers he thought were friends. Toward the end of the song, tired of life's struggles, Seger coos:

I began to find myself searchin'
Searchin' for shelter again and again
Against the wind
A little something against the wind
I found myself seeking shelter against the wind
Well those drifter's days are past me now
I've got so much more to think about
Deadlines and commitments

What to leave in, what to leave out
Against the wind
I'm still runnin' against the wind
I'm older now but still running
Against the wind[13]

To rise above the status quo, you must keep running against the wind. The trick is to align yourself with people moving in the same direction. Being in industries that are on the move—aviation and automotive—we've found a few examples we hope will illustrate how to lessen the forces against you.

Long before the Wright brothers dreamed that people could fly, philosophers studied birds. The V-shaped flight formation of geese took the inspiration one step (or nautical mile as we measure distance in aviation) further. In V formation, all the birds except the one in the lead fly in the upwash from the wingtip vortices of the bird ahead. Because the lead bird changes from time-to-time, all the birds can capitalize on energy saving efficiencies of air movement through the flock's corporate efforts. Similarly, aircraft—usually those involved in a combat situation—enjoy fuel efficiencies by flying close to each other.

Racecar drivers and cyclists also align in a close group to take advantage of the reduced drag from the slipstream. Successful drafting requires a tremendous amount of communication and cooperation between all of the moving parts. But ultimately, the efforts improve the velocity and performance of all participants. Planes, cars, and bikes go faster and further when they align with others going in the same direction. You can too!

As we shift our focus from personal growth to rising above the status quo in our families, teams, and communities, we need to examine how we can crush mediocrity by working together.

Henry Ford is probably best known for the automobile company that still bears his name, but it's the contribution that he made to business processes that changed the world. Ford was the first manufacturer to employ an assembly line. This revolutionary way of allowing employees to specialize and improve efficiencies shortened time-to-market for new products and also lowered the barrier-to-entry for ownership. This meant that a middle-class worker who built the car could also own one.

He was the first major employer to institute an eight-hour workday and pay wage-earners an unprecedented five dollars per day. This allowed him to attract and retain the best and brightest. Henry hired a diverse worker base and gave minorities and women more jobs than any employer in the area. He championed the working class and was a pioneer in profit sharing and franchising.

One of Henry's lesser-known accomplishments is his contribution to aviation. Despite his opposition to war, when the U.S. engaged in World War II in 1941, Henry built a factory specifically for manufacturing airplanes. This plant produced 9,000 B-24 bombers during the war—with an average of 650 per month at peak production. To put that in perspective, his single factory was producing *four times more* planes per year than are built in jet manufacturing plants *worldwide* today. Henry understood the principle of working together for a common goal.

> **Coming together is a beginning; keeping together is progress; working together is success.**
>
> –Henry Ford

"You will find men who don't seem to see that we must *all* lift together and pull together," he said. He was a master at getting people to work together. Henry's factory was a vital part of nearly 300,000 aircraft built in the U.S. between 1940 and 1945. During those years, aviation became the number one industry in the U.S. Consequently, the superior airpower and innovation of the Allies was a deciding factor in the outcome of World War II. This is a great example of millions of people rising together to crush not only mediocrity but also a global threat.

Stepping on Others to Get Ahead is Counter-Productive

In present times, we see people rallying together for short periods of time, such as cheering for the Denver Broncos' legendary quarterback Payton Manning to win an NFL Super Bowl even though their loyalties are typically with another team. Another example would be when people unite behind a political candidate for gender or ethnicity reasons. More often, people seem contentious and divisive rather than united for a common good. Sadly, this seems especially true of women.

As women, we particularly want to challenge you, our sisters, to operate *together*. Nineteenth-century English poet Matthew Arnold once said, "If there ever comes a time when the women of the world come together purely and simply for the benefit of mankind, it will be a force such as the world has never known."[14]

Unfortunately, instead of rallying behind a flagging sister, we judge, gossip, smirk, or inwardly cheer when a woman whose life looked better than ours messes up. According to the newly popular online dictionary, www. urbandictionary.com, someone like this is defined as a hater, "a person that simply cannot be happy for another person's success. So rather than be happy they make a point of exposing a flaw in that person."[15]

UrbanDictionary.com goes on to explain further: Hating, the result of being a hater, is not exactly jealousy. The hater doesn't want to be the person they hate. Rather, the hater wants to knock someone else down a notch.

It's time to stop this behavior and work together. We must find our tribe, that close group of friends who are loyal and care for each other like family. If we take a page from nature, we need only look at the king of the beasts and his pride to see this principle in action. Lions patrol their territory, challenging predators and establishing order in their pride.

Lionesses **collaborate** instead of **competing**. They hunt and provide for the pride as a team. They take turns watching for predators. They raise their young together, even nursing cubs not their own. They groom one another, removing parasites and licking matted fur and wounds.

What would it look like if women looked out for other women and collaborated? What if we cooperated when

> **If lionesses stop working as a team, the pride perishes.**

one of our children was acting up instead of gossiping or judging? What would happen in our communities if we defended our neighbors and confronted bad behavior? What would happen if we fully supported the women in our lives? If we truly want the best for our families and communities, doesn't it make sense to help each other become better?

What if rising together was the opposite of stepping on somebody else to get to the top of the heap? Wouldn't the foundation be stronger? Everyone needs to get involved. Women can be the catalyst for lasting change. It's time we live up to the wise words of Mathew Arnold and come together for the benefit of humanity. It may seem too much of a stretch for some, but if you feel that way we challenge you to broaden your vision of who you are and what you can do. Many women throughout history have done remarkable things. Together, we can too.

Overcoming Differences

Disney's movie *Zootopia* was released while we were writing this book. The setting of the movie is a world where predators and prey live in harmony, but prejudices still exist. One of the opening scenes lines up with our theme. Judy Hopps, a young female bunny, was determined to become a police officer. But the police force in the city of Zootopia consisted of much larger animals like elephants and rhinos. Little Judy would be no match for their brute strength. And her parents Stu and Bonnie discouraged her:

Stu: "You ever wonder how your mom and me got to be so darn happy?"

Judy: "Nope."

Stu: "Well, we gave up on our dreams and we settled. Right, Bonnie?"

Bonnie: "Oh yes, that's right, Stu, we settled. We settled hard."

Stu: "See, that's the beauty of complacency, Judy. If you don't try anything new, you'll never fail."

Judy: "I like trying actually."[16]

Little Judy not only tried and failed, but she also tried again and succeeded. She joined the police academy and figured out how to overcome her obstacles by using others' strengths. She bounced her way to finishing at the top of her class. However, when she got to her first assignment, she faced a new set of challenges and disappointments. As a result, the rabbit police officer ended up joining forces with a less-than-willing collaborator—a fox. As the two worked together, they discovered some stereotypes are true. Some are not.

The unlikely allies found, as they navigated the plot twists in their story, they were not so different after all. Without ruining the story for those of you who haven't seen it, their alliance, despite their biology, made the story outcome all the sweeter.

When we open our eyes to the strengths of those around us and set our bigotry and prejudices aside, we can find common goals and crush mediocrity together. If we stay in our limited circle, our legacy has a good chance of staying small.

Everyone Needs a Wingman

Sometimes we can feel as if we're stuck in the crux of an action-adventure film with pressures coming from every side. At those times, it's great to have a co-star who has our back—you know, the one with two pairs of night vision goggles and a body strapped with every weapon known to man? Life is a great adventure, and it's much easier to make it through successfully with a wingman, or in our case, a wing woman.

We all have blind spots, areas where we cannot see what's coming, even though others around us can. Having people around who care enough to point out the hazards in business and life can help us avoid disasters. Sometimes admitting that we are vulnerable, that we don't know it all or don't excel in everything, can lay the foundation to a great relationship. People like helping people. If someone projects that they never need help, they'll never get any. But those that seek help, guidance, or advice will find someone eager to be of assistance.

When René was selected for a profile in *JetSet* magazine several years ago, she called Lisa, even though they had only spoken a few times. While Lisa had a career in automotive, she also had studied fashion merchandising and had helped René pick out flattering outfits for a charity fashion show several years before. This particular day, they met at Neiman Marcus, a block from Lisa's dealership. Lisa put René in (of all colors) purple. René would never have picked it, but it's one of her favorites now. In the photo, the contrast of the purple with René's auburn hair and the white of the jet and the Ferrari, not to mention the red-bottomed shoes, was striking.

The point here isn't that Lisa helped René select clothes. It's that René knew Lisa had a keen eye for fashion and René asked for assistance. That call resulted in a great time shopping and rekindled a friendship, not to mention a killer outfit on a magazine's cover.

When we have room to celebrate each other's gifts and are willing to make each other better, we provide the environment for empowerment to take hold in our lives.

If Lisa had put René in a mediocre outfit because she was jealous that she wasn't on the cover of the magazine, the result would have been drastically different.

You may think that you would never sabotage someone else's success, but our society does tend to celebrate people's failures. If you've tried to climb the proverbial corporate ladder, you inevitably had people who opened a door—or who stood in your way, stepped on your fingers, or stabbed you in the back. Our careers, our workplaces, and our communities all improve when we root for one another and build each other up.

Root for Each Other

One of the episodes of *I Love Lucy* always makes us laugh. It's the one where Lucy and her best friend Ethel work in a candy factory.[17] It may well be Lucille Ball's most famous skit. Their supervisor puts them on an assembly line wrapping chocolates as a final resort to save their jobs. She tells them if any of the chocolates get by unwrapped, they will be fired.

The candy starts to come out slowly and well-spaced out on a conveyer belt. Lucy and Ethel each pick up a piece from the conveyor belt, wrap it, and set it back down. "This is easy," Lucy says. Ethel agrees they can handle the job.

Suddenly the candy starts coming faster. They have to pull a few off of the conveyor belt. Lucy eats a piece. So does Ethel. When they have their mouths stuffed and a pile of chocolates in front of them, they hear the supervisor coming. They quickly stuff chocolates in their blouses and chef hats. The audience roars with laughter. The supervisor enters the scene, tells them good job, and then yells to whoever controls the tempo of the conveyor belt to speed it up.

Obviously, Lucy and Ethel fail in the job, so it's not a story about achieving an objective. But it is a story of sticking together and rooting for each other. These two friends did everything in their power to wrap the chocolates and work together for a common goal. Neither of them blamed the other or complained to the supervisor about the other person. That's the beauty of finding people on the same path as you. If, for whatever reason you fail, at least you're not alone. If you succeed, the victory is sweeter because it was shared. Chocolate factory, here we come.

We All Need Accountability

The other benefit of having people involved in your life is accountability. We tend to shy away from this word and the censure we believe it brings. But accountability is one of the key ingredients in crushing mediocrity.

Early in 2016, Lisa had accomplished everything she could with the Fiat dealership in Austin. She had broken the North American sales records. The dealership had earned two best workplace awards. They had carried the number one dealership title almost every year. In addition, **Automotive News** named Lisa as one of the top 100 women in automotive. **Austin Business Journal** deemed her one of the most powerful women in the Texas capital. She had served on Fiat Chrysler Automobiles' National Dealer Council for four years. She had nowhere to grow with her current platform.

As Lisa received award after award, René challenged Lisa to take the next step in revolutionizing the culture of the automotive industry for consumers and workers (especially women) because she had declared that as her purpose in returning to the industry. Lisa toyed with starting a female-friendly car-buying service. She got involved with Cox Automotive as their beta site for Flex Drive, a subscription-based alternative to car ownership that offers late model, fuel-efficient vehicles for use by the week or month.

But they both knew Lisa had a bigger stage to take. René kept pressing. Finally, Lisa realized she couldn't change the status quo of an entire industry and continue running a dealership day-to-day. René started asking Lisa whether she had negotiated her buyout, written a resignation letter, and planned her next steps.

René's persistence in holding Lisa accountable to her underlying purpose gave Lisa the courage to take a leap of faith to equip thousands of women and men to crush mediocrity, redefine an industry, and leave their world a better place.

Without daily accountability to take the small steps, and the focus of accountability to keep the bigger picture in mind, Lisa would still be the general manager of Fiat/Alfa Romeo of Austin. Oh sure, she would be winning awards and breaking records, but she wouldn't be happy with the degree of change she was making in the industry from her six-day-a-week desk job. Along with René's help, the key was Lisa's willingness to be held accountable.

You need to *want* to excel in every part of your life, find others who feel the same way, open up to them, admit you need help when you do, be there for others, hold each other accountable, and stay on the course to rise together. It sounds difficult, but it isn't insurmountable, especially not when you focus on the reward of a better life for you and those around you.

6
Stand Out

If we don't challenge the way things are,
we are destined to drift in a river of mediocrity,
never rising above the status quo.

Stop Praising Mediocrity

There is probably nothing that either of us criticizes more than the idea of participation trophies. The plastic cups and stands and figurines themselves are not the issue. In fact, we applaud the marketing genius who has become rich overselling trophies to every little league team and spelling bee coordinator in the country. It's a good way to capitalize on everyone's need to feel special, both for little Johnny and his parents. The problem is, participation trophies do more harm than good.

In American society, we are sending convoluted and mixed messages in our schools.

Participation trophies dilute the accomplishments of the victors and instead celebrate mediocrity.

On one hand, we are changing policies so that we no longer label kids with failure. We give accolades to kids for showing up at the countless events in elementary and even middle school. Yet as these same kids approach adulthood, we expect them to *want* to excel in school, to win competitions, and to qualify for scholarships. We are frustrated when these things are not important to them. We have praised kids into mediocrity, and the sudden real-life pressures to excel can be overwhelming for them. Further, this lowering of expectations is finding its way into college graduation criteria, job performance requirements, and public opinion.

Spend a warm fall evening in a high school football stadium in Texas, and you'll hear the, um, "participation" of parents and fans on the same students as they drop balls or miss tackles. In professional sports, mere participation is not an option. Coaches are fired for losing. Franchises are sold and moved to different cities. Ticket sales plummet. Athletes lose their jobs.

It's no wonder millennials entering the workforce are confused. Do they get an A for effort or are they required to perform for promotion? Do they get a do-over when they make a mistake that costs their employer millions of dollars or do they get fired, maybe even prosecuted? Do they believe the Woody Allen quote: "Eighty percent of success is showing up" or can they look at his life and realize that Woody Allen never "just showed up" to anything? Imagine if that's all it took to win four Academy Awards. They'd be dust collectors in a basement somewhere. Participation trophies.

Recognize True Success

Muirfield Village Golf Club, in Dublin, Ohio, is the home of the annual Memorial Tournament and its founder, Jack Nicklaus. For more than six decades, Jack has been crushing drives, crushing records, and crushing mediocrity at every turn. While most of Jack's trophies are on display for the public at his museum on the grounds of the Ohio State University, the keepsakes from a few of his most memorable wins occupy an entire wall at MVGC. The stairway leading to the clubhouse pro shop hosts all of the *Sports Illustrated* covers on which he was featured.

Jack stands out as the most celebrated professional golfer of all time, an exceptional business leader, the most sought-after golf course designer in the world, and a man of great values. René's husband Curt applied to become a member at Muirfield Village several years ago. He was surprised with all of Jack's accomplishments, his criteria for granting membership, which he does personally, are much more about character than accomplishments or golf skills. That's because Jack knows that truly standing out comes from within.

Jack's life is a testament of this belief in action. He has competed in thousands of golf tournaments. He played in a record 154 consecutive Major tournaments (each year the Masters, the U.S. Open, the Open Championship, and the

> **"Achievement is largely the product of steadily raising one's levels of aspiration and expectation. "**
> –Jack Nicklaus

PGA Championship) between 1957 and 1998. He finished in the top 10 in less than half of these contests. He took home only 18 first-place trophies. And with all those "failures," Jack Nicklaus remains the winningest professional golfer of all time. Consistency, perseverance, and the goal of building a legacy are mainstays in Jack's life. His chosen career is a perfect example to us that there is room in life to stand out, even when you don't always win the trophy.

Recognition is a powerful motivator. Trophies have served for centuries as a clear symbol of achievement.

Let's not cheapen them by passing them out freely. Let's teach each generation that truly earned recognition comes from trying hard, failing, getting back up again, and trying harder as many times as necessary. The more difficult the fight for the reward, the more meaningful the trophy.

Don't Be Afraid of Rocking the Boat

Coco Chanel once said, "In order to be irreplaceable, one must always be different." She was definitely that. The brand she created remains iconic more than 45 years after her death. One of the richest women of all time, Coco utilized jersey and tweed fabrics in her designs, doing away with corsets (hallelujah) and introducing a sportier and casually chic style of clothing, along with perfumes, handbags, and jewelry. *Time* magazine named Coco one of the 100 most influential people of the 20th century.[18] She stood out.

Lisa is well known for breaking records with her Fiat dealership, but she hasn't always focused on cars. With a degree in fashion merchandising, she keeps tabs on the retail market and loves fashion and textiles. She loves the business of clothes, shoes, and accessories, and she's a student of how things are sold in retail—especially to women. In fact, when Lisa re-entered the automotive business in 2009, it was as a consultant for improving sales to women.

Her vision was to make the car-buying experience more fun for females (not to mention other disenfranchised buyers). She believed the U.S. economy could be revitalized by women upgrading their vehicles rather than driving them till the wheels fell off. Research supported her observations; males changed vehicles more than twice as frequently as females on average. Women polled indicated that they preferred having a root canal to a buying a car. With 85 percent of buying decisions made or strongly influenced by women, Lisa knew she could be wildly successful if she could capture that market. The reintroduction of the Fiat brand to the U.S. gave her an even bigger opportunity.

Drawing on her retail experience, Lisa put her showroom in an upscale shopping area. It was the first time an auto retailer had Apple, Tiffany's, and Louis Vuitton as neighbors. From that store and her success with female buyers, Lisa took the bold risk of saying she was going to be the number one dealer in the country. Mind you, her dealership was in the heart of Texas, the largest pickup truck market in the world. Lisa was so sure of her team and their strategy, she even challenged Fiat CEO Tim Kuniskis to a wager that she would break sales records and close more than 100 new car transactions in a single month. If she did, Tim would have to bring Sergio Marchionne, the CEO of Fiat Chrysler Automobiles (FCA), to her store.

At the time, Sergio had never visited a dealership in the U.S. In April 2012, Lisa's team, from their 6,000-square-foot showroom with a red carpet running through the center, delivered their 111th Fiat 500 of the month. The press started calling. Tim Kuniskis panicked because he hadn't told Sergio about the bet. He offered to fly in Academy Award winning actor George Clooney instead. Lisa thanked him for the offer but told him to fire up Sergio's jet. She would settle for nothing less than the boss. And as everyone in the automotive industry knows, a deal is a deal.

Lisa stood out in her decision to open a dealership in a nontraditional fashion. She stood out by setting a public and lofty goal for her sales team. She also stood out in her Italian suit (strongly "suggested" by Fiat's press team) as one of the most influential men in the automotive world walked the red carpet in her small, record-breaking Texas showroom to congratulate her.

Because Lisa stood out and broke records, the man in charge of the Fiat, Ferrari, Maserati, Alfa Romeo, Jeep, Chrysler, Dodge, Ram, and Abarth brands appointed her to join 17 men on the dealer council. Standing out skyrocketed Lisa's career in automotive. Sergio didn't visit all his dealerships. Only Lisa had earned the recognition and the first place trophy. The others, though they also sold cars, got to see pictures of Sergio and Lisa. To the winner go the spoils.

Be Purposeful

You must start with a goal in mind. Your *why* must be strong enough to hold you steady, because you will have opposition, especially if you are trying to stand out, start something new, or go against the grain.

When René and her husband started Charlie Bravo, they knew they would be competing against companies that had been in business 30 years or more, companies with good names and long client lists. René's goal was to make her company stand out amidst giants and to stay in business as a newcomer in a tough market. She designed the company logo to resemble the nose art from a WWII bomber, both to pay tribute to the men and women who had ensured her future with their sacrifices and to communicate more longevity than they actually had. The name and the logo together were meant to convey René and Curt's dedication to the work ethic and values of the 1940s and 50s when a handshake was even more important than a legal document.

René wanted to stand out—and she has. However, it's important to note that when someone chooses to stand out, those who reflect the status quo may be judgmental. One major advertising site refused to let her use the iconic part of the logo in her ads, and a few industry leaders have criticized the calendar she created as a marketing piece with modest pin-up girls and warbirds. René didn't buckle under their pressure. Because her brand was so different, even when Charlie Bravo was a fledgling company, people around the world began to recognize the brand—and the redheaded woman behind it.

There are perks to being a woman in a room full of men in our respective industries. And there are benefits to being excellent in a sea of average. We aren't apologetic about taking advantage of opportunities to raise the bar, stand out, and crush mediocrity.

Start with the Small Things

We believe excellence is a key to crushing mediocrity and standing out. Attention to detail and willingness to excel in menial things will build the foundation for something great in the future.

An example we can all relate to is Lego, the company that makes interlocking, multi-colored plastic building blocks and has grown into a worldwide brand.

> **If you don't lay the foundation correctly and solidly, it will be impossible to sustain someting spectacular.**

Despite variation from the original design and the ever-changing purposes of the individual pieces, each block remains compatible in some way with existing pieces. Lego bricks from 1958 still interlock with those made today. Per company manifesto, each Lego piece must be fabricated to an exacting degree of precision. The machines that manufacture Lego bricks have tolerances as small as 10 micrometers. That's one hundredth of a millimeter—or about 10 percent of the width of a human hair for those of you, like us, who have forgotten your elementary school lessons on metric measurements.

Lego has built an empire by excelling in the small things. In fact, in February 2015, according to *Brand Fi-*

nance, Lego overtook Ferrari (sorry, Sergio) as the most powerful brand in the world.[19] Attention to detail and consistency in the small things translates to a powerful foundation for growth.

Consider this example. When René's kids were younger, she received a phone call from her neighbor, Meredith, who was the president of the Parent Teacher Association at René's son's middle school. Meredith asked if René could help with the PTA, something she had purposefully avoided. She was willing to do just about anything for her kids, but thought getting involved with the PTA was for supermoms on Adderall who over-achieved at everything. One day, as chance would have it, Meredith managed to corner her neighbor when René went to get her mail.

After sensing her reluctance, Meredith promised René she wouldn't have to come to meetings; she could just run the school store. It was open one day a week and losing money every year, not what you would call a high-profile assignment. They just needed it to break even. René agreed and applied her standard of excellence to the project. She launched a new vision and turned the losing proposition into the biggest fundraiser for the PTA, earning a $10,000 profit in the first year using 25 parents and 45 students as volunteers. She did it by paying attention to excellence in the small things—pencils, bouncy balls (much to the principals' chagrin) and locker mirrors.

Today, running a multi-million-dollar company, she drives her co-workers a little bit crazy with deadlines and high standards and logo guidelines and sentence structure corrections, but they do appreciate it when sales increase.

Because they are excellent in the small things, Charlie Bravo Aviation stands out as one of the best-marketed aircraft brokers in the world. They are in the top 10 companies of their type worldwide.

Stand *for* Something

Standing out requires that you take risks, take action, think outside the box, build upon successes *and* failures, and refuse to give up. But even those things are not enough. If you truly want to stand out, you must figure out what you stand for.

As you know by now, Lisa stands out in just about everything she does. Part of her charm is in being able to sell anything. It's easy for her to connect with people and sell a product or service she knows will benefit them. To her chagrin, René figured this out at a Girl Scout Women of Distinction luncheon several years ago. Lisa was an honoree, and she was also making a pitch to get people from the audience involved in STEM (science, technology, engineering, and math) initiatives.

Lisa's presentation started with a $300 sales plug for a local program for girls to have experiential exposure to STEM. The luncheon ended with a three-year, $3,000 pledge "opportunity" to build the national program developed by Anna Maria Chavez, the Girl Scout USA President, to equip more girls with opportunities for education, and even careers, in fields not traditionally pursued by women. René jokes that Lisa sold her a $3,300 box of Thin Mints at lunch that day, but the truth is she was happy to contribute.

Lisa's mantra at Fiat was always, "It's not what you sell; it's what you stand for." She has found her success in living out that philosophy. In a state with as many Ford F-150s as longhorn cattle, selling Fiats was not a sure thing. But Lisa didn't just build a dynamic team; she also built an engaging culture. She empowered her employees and her buyers, invested in her community, and even added philanthropic events. Her Fiat/Alfa Romeo dealership in Austin was a prominent venue for many charity event coordinators.

It's because of what Lisa stands for that her employees were teary-eyed (yes, even a few men) when she announced she was selling her equity in the dealership to her business partner. Their sadness was in losing a leader who believed in them and gave them opportunities to be part of something bigger. Lisa stands for team and community and championing the underdog. She stands for treating people right and going the extra mile. These things are the foundation of Lisa's beliefs—and they make her stand out.

When you lead from a place of conviction and boldness, your employees and teammates will rally around you and stick with you through thick and thin. You can make excuses about why you blend in, or you can do what it takes to rise above the status quo. It's time to figure out what you believe in and what you can do to take a stand. Once you've laid the foundation, you'll be able to build a beautiful life that others will notice. Will you take the first step? Stand up, then stand out? We're rooting for you!

7
Repurpose Your Fears

We can crush mediocrity by repurposing our fears to propel us into the right actions.

Regardless of what we've been through, how strong we are, or what we know, we're all afraid of something. Our fears can result from actual experiences or they can be born from our insecurities. No one is immune; we just fear different things.

To illustrate, René has a 100-pound American Bulldog, named Bazooka. As you may know, this is a breed recognized for its strength, stoicism and protectiveness. He indeed has a ferocious bark and a menacing profile, yet Bazooka is a snuggler, and sometimes appears to be more fearful than fearsome. When someone wears a hat or carries in a plant, Bazooka retreats. If something new is on the patio, he will refuse to go out, even to play.

This tough, intimidating pup tucks his tail and backs away at the sight of a mop bucket, and, no, we don't think it's a male gender bias. So how does this bucket-fearing puppy terrify a dinner guest who is seven-feet tall, weighs 250 pounds, and "makes buckets" for a living as a professional basketball player? Well, Youssou Ndoye grew up in Senegal, where big dogs are not household pets. They are wild animals.

While we don't think a fear of buckets or dogs is going to derail you, there are fears that will. And your reaction to them is very real.

According to Wikipedia the fight-or-flight response[20] to a perceived harmful event, or threat to survival is a physiological reaction, identical to that in nature, priming the animal for fighting or fleeing. We don't live in a jungle; we live in a civilized world. Most of our fears aren't due to threats of our very survival. Our fears are more mental or emotional. Our imagination takes us to a possible future where the worst has happened, and we are humiliated or impoverished somehow. These fears cause many of us to flee or freeze, either running away from our calling or remaining stagnant. Some things are certainly worth fighting for.

Wouldn't it be powerful if we could turn our fears into something positive? What if we allow the fear of failure to motivate us to keep going when we feel like giving up? What if we turn the fear of rejection into a determination to persist? What if we repurpose the fear of change to fuel our excitement about

> **"Everything you want is on the other side of fear."**
> –Jack Canfield, author *Chicken Soup for the Soul*

new opportunities? What if we turn our fear of falling short into a vulnerability that helps others grow? What if we stop being intimidated by how other people see us and turn our fear of inadequacy into honest introspection and celebrate our strengths?

Refuse to be Paralyzed by a Fear of Failure

We talk more about recovering from failure in the next chapter, but here we just want to address the fact that past failures can immobilize you. They can play with your head and keep you stagnant. When you have a history of failing in a certain area, the fear of failing again can become downright paralyzing.

Ingrid Vanderveldt has had good reason to fear failure. She describes herself as a serial entrepreneur, and she has started several companies, not all of which were successful. After selling two small companies when she was in her 20s, she jumped into a venture she was passionate about, and as she put it, the company became a money pit. It drained her of all her capital and eventually failed, leaving her broke and homeless.

While she feared to fail again, Ingrid didn't allow those experiences to define her. Instead, she followed the lead of other successful entrepreneurs she knew: leveraging and learning from that failure as part of her journey to becoming one of the most highly regarded female entrepreneurs in the world. Drawing deeply upon her faith, Ingrid chose to propel herself forward, albeit a bit more cautiously.

She said, "From that experience, I learned the importance of setting up a financial plan and being the architect of building a business. Getting knocked down and finding myself against a wall was very humbling. Fortunately for me, I wasn't alone. I had an incredible support network that helped me move past this failure and get back on my feet.

"I often tell other entrepreneurs that failing is part of the process. If you haven't failed at something, especially doing something you love, you probably aren't innovating enough. You should be concerned when everything is going perfectly because you have probably become too comfortable. Before you know what's happening, things become stagnant, and your competition moves past you. Keep innovating and find peace in knowing that the most successful entrepreneurs around the globe have also had their moments of failure, and you are simply joining this amazing tribe of leaders."

Ingrid knows what she's talking about. After her stint in poverty, she went on to launch many different companies while also investing in a few others. She hosted the first ever prime-time business television series for CNBC and became the first Entrepreneur-in-Residence at Dell, helping others navigate entrepreneurship. Later, she was appointed as a member of the United Nations Foundation's Global Entrepreneurship Council.

These days, she can be found leading her new passion, EBW 2020 (Empowering a Billion Women by 2020), through which she hopes to equip a billion women in developing countries with mobile technology, financial literacy, and business mentoring. Not only has she moved past her fear of failure, Ingrid and her other equally passionate colleagues are willing to help other women navigate the failures inherent in rising above the status quo.

In her defining moment, Ingrid pressed on, knowing that if she survived it once, she could certainly survive it again. So even if you've failed before, try and try again. Change your tactics. Realign your team. Take the risk. The sky's the limit.

Embrace The Fact That Change Can Be Good

Dr. Spencer Johnson's book *Who Moved My Cheese?*[21] is an encouraging and thought-provoking resource for those facing change. It's a parable that shows how four different characters handle a shift in resources. The two mice, Sniff and Scurry, remain nimble and handle the depletion of their cheese supply without much angst. The two little people, Hem and Haw, with a reasonable supply, become complacent, build a life around their resources, and delay making changes when their circumstances change.

The book is a lighthearted exposé on the different reactions to change and how we can handle them appropriately. It's an easy read, and with more than 26,000,000 copies sold worldwide, you should be able to find a copy in your local library or maybe on the bookshelf of a friend who has successfully navigated a transition. Change isn't always bad, even when it appears to be. Being able to adapt to new circumstances is a trait you should activate.

As a parent, getting a call at two in the morning and hearing that your 19-year-old son has had an accident at a fraternity house and is being loaded into an ambulance ignites indescribable fear. There is nothing trivial about this type of fear; it grips the heart. The drive to the hospital, not knowing his condition, is one of life's scariest moments.

This happened to Lisa and James with their son JT. Although his initial prognosis was paralysis, Lisa and James did not allow panic to paralyze them. They prayed, called in every favor, summoned the best specialists in the country, and explored every option. They turned their fear into acceptance of a "new normal" and made plans to move their son, who had been in firefighting school at Texas A&M, back into their home with his new physical limitations.

Miraculously, they didn't need the nurses and occupational therapists, nor the architect and construction crew that they had begun arranging. Two weeks after that fateful night, JT began moving again and experienced a full, inexplicable recovery.

When fear of change threatens to overwhelm you, concentrate on what the new normal will bring about, and begin planning how you can be successful in that place. For Lisa's family, it was to take care of JT as a paraplegic. For you, or someone you know who is crippled by the fear of change, it may be a new job or a new relationship, or a move to a new city. You can do it.

Turn Fear of Rejection into Determination to Persist

Back when we were kids, we both sold Girl Scout cookies door-to-door. We'd canvas the neighborhood in our uniforms with the little green sashes. Most neighbors would invite us in, order a few boxes, and ask us how school was going that year. Nobody was carb-conscious back then, so most people ordered at least one box, and if they didn't want cookies, they typically just didn't answer the door.

Today, those girls get a first-hand taste of what it feels like to have a real sales job. Due to changing policies, instead of canvassing their neighborhoods, they now must stand in front of a local retailer with a table and a couple of moms, with boxes and boxes of cookies to sell to all who pass by.

Those of us who have already bought five boxes and hidden them in the freezer, so our husband doesn't get into them might enter the exit to avoid the table. Or we just say, "no, we've already bought some," or we might avoid eye contact altogether. Maybe we tell them we will buy some on the way out, and then conveniently forget or wait for others to exit so that we can sneak by in the crowd. We can't imagine what some of those shy little darlings think when their turn comes up to man the sales table. But that pressure—and yes, even rejection—prepares Girl Scouts to handle adult situations early on.

In higher-stakes sales jobs, we face some of the same obstacles the Girl Scouts do. People avoid us, voice objections, screen calls, or have someone else run interference. Selling big-ticket items that involve prospecting sometimes means 1,000 negative responses before there is one that results in a commission check. That's a lot of rejection.

While you'll certainly avoid rejection if you don't ask, that fear can limit the positive responses to absolutely zilch. Girl Scouts don't quit because someone doesn't buy cookies. They learn how to handle the negative and keep going despite the rejection. If Girl Scouts can face it, so can you. The stakes might be higher, but then so are the rewards.

> **Facing the fear of rejection builds confidence.**

If fear of rejection is an issue for you, make sure to surround yourself with people who can help you overcome it, as discussed in the Operate Together chapter. This type of fear is a killer, and it's not just your future at stake.

As parents, our fear of rejection projects itself onto our kids, causing them to lack confidence in the classroom, on the playground, and in difficult situations. As business leaders, we can cripple our co-workers by stifling enthusiasm and the willingness to take risks. Eventually, we have to choose to handle rejection from other people instead of compromising our dreams or failing to fulfill our purpose.

Squash the Fear of Success

Most of us can admit when we have a fear of failure, or change, or rejection. But we rarely recognize we are afraid of success. It manifests in a number of ways that others can see, but you usually cannot. Here are a few telltale signs you may be suffering from achievemephobia.

- You have the same dream you had three years ago, and you aren't any closer to achieving it. Lisa dreamed of being a motivational speaker for years—even had a renowned speaking coach—before she hired an agent or listed her keynote speeches on a speaker's website. Now she's offered speaking engagements all over the world.

- You feel guilty about any success you have, no matter how small, because your friends, family, or co-workers haven't had the same success. And you certainly don't want them to think you're putting on airs, gloating, or becoming critical of their lack of drive, skills or lucky breaks. There's a fine line we walk, which is why it is important to align ourselves with others who are going the same direction.

• You don't complete projects, either at work or at home. Are you a person who thrives on lists, detailing the steps and then failing to complete that last item that would take you across the finish line at a sprint? Do you talk about what you are going to do but then fail to see it through? Make a commitment to finishing and then do it!

• You compromise your own goals or agenda to avoid conflict in a group—or even conflict within your family. This is different than sacrificing for your children or the good of the group. When you abandon dreams to further your education or pursue a promotion because you would have to ask others to sacrifice with you because it might cause conflict, this might be your barrier to rising above the status quo. Compromise shouldn't be one-sided, especially when your purpose or your dreams are at stake.

• You talk yourself out of your dreams by convincing yourself that you're not good enough to achieve them. Or, you subconsciously feel that you don't deserve to enjoy success in your life. But if not you, then who really does? This is particularly true of women—just look at the continued disparity between salaries for women and men doing the same job with the same skill set or education.

• You believe that if you do achieve success, you won't be able to sustain it. The price of success can be high. Your life will be under a microscope all of the time. The pressure is greater, and it can definitely be lonely at the top. Our friend Rhoda Mae Kerr gives a picture of the antithesis of this point. She became a firefighter in her 30s, grew in leadership and sought a chief position for five years before she convinced someone to take a chance on her. She finally earned a major metropolitan market position in Austin, and became the first female President and Chair of the Board of Directors of the International Association of Fire Chiefs. Was it hard? Yes. Was it worth it? Yes, again. Rhoda Mae willingly pays the price to blaze a trail for other men and women to pursue their dreams.

Don't get in the way of your own success. If you are stalling your rise to the top of wherever you are going, stop it, reassess, and move on. Finish the to-do list. Compromise with others, not with yourself. And, for goodness sakes, stop telling yourself you're not good enough. Who is going to change the world if not you?

Do Not Let Others' Opinions Derail You

Lisa Bevere is one of the boldest people we know. She speaks out about injustices; she champions women in countries where it's unpopular to promote women's rights. And she fearlessly tells it like she sees it. But that wasn't always the case.

Lisa's story is one of *overcoming* her fears. In high school, she was required to take either speech or debate to graduate. No prospect could have frightened her more. She said, "As a teenager, I was terrified of getting up in front of people. I had lost an eye to a form of cancer called retinoblastoma when I was five years old. Overnight, life as I'd known it changed. I went from being confident and outgoing to being sullen and withdrawn. I felt that people no longer saw me. I watched as they tried to determine which eye they should look at when they spoke to me. At school, compliments changed to name-calling. I was dubbed 'One Eye' and 'Cyclops.'"

The day she had to give her first speech in high school was a disaster. Her fear was so great that she physically couldn't speak. The teacher gave her the opportunity to walk out of the classroom and start again, but she chose not to. Instead, she ran to the guidance counselor's office. He was sympathetic to Lisa's handicap, and not just for speech class. He also let her opt out of typing, which was difficult with limited vision.

She had study hall instead of typing and a literature course in the place of speech class, but it was just a reprieve. As she became an adult, she ended up learning the lessons in a much tougher environment, a stage onto which her loving husband repeatedly pushed her, one that eventually helped her overcome her fears.

Today, as the best-selling author of more than a dozen books, all of which she typed herself, and as one of the most highly sought after female Christian speakers in the world, Lisa is pretty much fearless. Nobody looks more comfortable on stage than Lisa Bevere. She faced her fear of public speaking, her fear of looking foolish, her fear of being the focus of people's attention, even when she could only focus on them with one eye. The fear that finally drove Lisa to succeed was the fear that she would miss her destiny.

Give More Weight to Your Dreams than Your Fears

When you finally face your fears, you figure out that the worst thing that can happen isn't failure or rejection or being exposed as inadequate or a new normal that you didn't choose.

The worst thing that can happen is completely missing the opportunities that give your life significance. Those things that influence, empower, encourage, or motivate others to emulate your example are far more important than fear, no matter how real or big your fears may seem.

Like Lisa Bevere, you must harness the power in your fears into something positive. Turn the fear of rejection into a determination not to take no for an answer. Repurpose the fear of failure in a business venture to a conviction that quitting is not an option. Turn the fear of change into excitement because that excitement can fuel new opportunities. Redirect your deepest fears into a vulnerability that helps others grow. Your life story doesn't have to be dictated by anyone's opinion of you. Do not fear criticism.

"I've heard there are troubles of more than one kind; some come from ahead, and some come from behind. But I've brought a big bat. I'm all ready, you see; now my troubles are going to have troubles with me."
–Dr. Seuss

You crush mediocrity by facing your fears and repurposing them into something that triggers positive action—on a daily basis if necessary—with the bigger purpose and the bolder dream in mind. Like Sharon Lechter said in the foreword, ask "why not?"

8
Recover from Failure

Mediocrity is worse than failure.

We grew up listening to Paul Harvey's famous broadcasts themed *The Rest of the Story*. For more than six decades, Paul began his stories with little-known facts on a variety of subjects with a key element omitted until the end, when he revealed the rest of the story, usually the name of a well-known person or event. His presentations served as a constant reminder that success can (and usually does) come after facing a major obstacle or failure.

The biggest success on the heels of failure in documented history is probably the Christian faith. Whether you believe in the Bible or not, there is no denying that Christianity has successfully spread and grown throughout the last 2,000 years. With an estimated 2.2 billion followers, Christianity is the largest organization in the world.[22] However, its unlikely start with a group of 12 commoners and a 30-year-old wanderer seemed doomed to failure when its leader, Jesus Christ, died a criminal's death and his followers scattered in fear.

According to the Bible, after Christ rose from the dead and appeared to his disciples, they began the early church. Constant persecution forced these Christians and their converts to move from their lands, thus spreading the gospel throughout civilization. Clearly, before we consider something to be a failure, we need to know the rest of the story. What may appear to be a failure from one viewpoint could be seen as the beginning of success from another perspective.

If we are to rise from mediocrity, we cannot allow failures or setbacks to hold us back for the rest of our lives. The loss of a relationship, an unprofitable year, or a failed business may determine the turn in the path that we take, but we must rise above our circumstances and continue moving. Things that seem like failures today can be the launching pad for incredible turnarounds and spectacular finishes in the future. To achieve success from failure, we must learn from it and use it to accelerate ourselves to a different place. Otherwise, we end up losers in a repetitive cycle of failing again, stuck perpetually in mediocrity or worse.

Perhaps the types of failures that hurt most are the ones where we knew better and still made the stupid mistake—often for instant gratification—that affected our family, our workplace, or our community. Extramarital affairs, accidents caused by texting while driving, and living beyond our means all have devastating ripple effects.

Even when we make things right, forgiving ourselves for making the mistake in the first place can be difficult and often cripples us from making healthy decisions in the future. Guilt can freeze us in that place in time when we were at our worst. This is when failure morphs from the professor that can teach us a lesson to the warden that imprisons us. We must make a conscious decision to go on, while also putting safeguards in place to avoid that failure again.

Accept that Failure is Part of Success

If you have experience with failures or setbacks in business, you are not alone. According to several sources, 8 out of 10 entrepreneurs who start businesses fail. No matter if that statistic is accurate or skewed, if everyone who failed the first time just gave up, the world would be a completely different place.

Walt Disney was fired from the **Kansas City Star** newspaper because his editor felt he "lacked imagination and had no good ideas." He lost several businesses in the animation field for lack of money, was swindled by a distributor, which caused him to lose all his employees, and then had trouble selling his early Mickey Mouse animations.[23] Without Walt Disney's determination, our childhoods would have been significantly different.

Colonel Sanders, of Kentucky Fried Chicken fame, lost several jobs and his law practice by brawling with colleagues. He was well versed in changing jobs. By the time he was 30, he'd worked as a farmer, painter, teamster, blacksmith's helper, railway custodian, fireman, train conductor, lawyer, life insurance salesman, and a ferryboat company owner. It wasn't until he was in his 60s that the restaurateur franchised the concept of his special-recipe fried chicken and found his success.[24] Even in retirement, he didn't give up.

Oprah Winfrey, the richest African American of the 20th century, was not raised with a silver spoon in her mouth. Despite a troubled childhood, by 19, she was the first African American woman to anchor the news in Nashville. Her position didn't last though. She was fired because of her sincere compassion; her voice trembled when she reported a decrease of stock rates or another hurricane devastating a coastline. Her determination not to change her heartfelt style revolutionized the media industry. Eventually, she was invited to host a low-rated half-hour morning talk show in Chicago.[25] The rest, as they say, is history.

Thomas Edison possibly is the most illustrious example of failure—and success—in modern history.

Amid thousands of failures, Edison's inventions that did succeed launched new industries. Without electric light, utility power distribution, sound recording, and motion pictures, Oprah Winfrey, Walt

> **"I have not failed 10,000 times. I've successfully found 10,000 ways that will not work."**
> –*Thomas Edison*

Disney, nor any of the other people we've mentioned in this book would have built the legacy they did.

"Our greatest weakness lies in giving up," Edison said. "The most certain way to succeed is always to try just one more time." Failure can be a stepping-stone if you use it in the right way.

Learn from Your Mistakes and Failures

Several years after René and Curt started Charlie Bravo Aviation, René decided to start a sister company, which she named Charlie Bravo Charter. She built a team, fashioned a sisterly looking brand, and began selling private charter. Her advertisements caught the eye of a new company in town that had big-name investors and a lot of international media attention, Circuit of the Americas (COTA).

Most international tourists thought of Houston or Dallas when Texas came up in conversation, but COTA was putting Austin on the map. The organization was bringing Formula One back to the United States after a long hiatus by building a racetrack on the outskirts of Austin to host the U.S. Grand Prix. René saw a potential partnership with COTA as a feather in her cap, a way to gain media attention and secure a good reputation among charter operators and clients alike.

Contract negotiations took nearly six months. But Charlie Bravo Charter was finally named the official charter partner of the first Grand Prix in Austin in July 2012 with the race scheduled just four short months later. The company would provide charter on fixed wing aircraft into and out of Austin, as well as helicopter shuttles between downtown and the racetrack, which was expected to be a popular alternative to congested roads.

The Charlie Bravo team launched into action, securing helicopters and hiring an experienced operations team to make sure things ran smoothly on the three days of the race event with 18 different helicopters in operation. René learned more than she ever thought she would about helicopters, including how much room they need to take off and what helicopter pilots see as dangerous operational conditions.

She had a crash course in helipad approval and helicopter operations over commercial airports, since the Austin-Bergstrom International Airport was situated directly between downtown and the track—just five nautical miles from the city and two from the racetrack. She worked with the air traffic controllers at the Austin airport to make sure there would be no interference and coordinated with the FAA to expedite the approval of two new helipads in the Austin area.

René also navigated the politics of neighborhood associations that didn't want helicopter noise and FAA departments that didn't want to allow hot refueling, a practice that allows helicopters to be refueled with the engines still on and rotors still rotating.

Contractually promised first right of refusal on all the landing slots at the racetrack's six helipads, Charlie

Bravo Charter began taking reservations from VIPs and dignitaries all over the world. Passengers were color-coded by COTA based on the amount of money they had spent with the organization, and five different takeoff points were identified.

René met with the company that was going to oversee the helipad construction and direct helicopter traffic on the days of the event, and the company's principal, Steve Henry, agreed to mentor her, as he had been coordinating helicopter traffic for years at races. It ended up being a miracle he was able to help at all. Three months before the race, a car smashed into Steve when he stopped to help a stranded motorist. He spent six weeks fighting for his life in intensive care before starting rehab. The race weekend was his first outing, and it proved to be a doozy.

In the week before the race, several things happened. The operations company René had hired several months before backed out with no notice and no reason. In desperation, René called the assistant chief helicopter pilot for the state of Texas. He rounded up some officers who could help with walkie-talkies and cool composure. A helicopter pilot recently retired from the U.S. Army volunteered to take over the helicopter operations for the busiest helipad.

If René wasn't under enough pressure, just a few days before the race, the City of Austin decided that no helicopter operations could take place after dark in the city, even with proper lighting. With the race ending at 4:30 in the afternoon just a month before the shortest day of the year, René had to make a decision to transport all of the downtown passengers to the Austin airport and provide limos to take them back to the city rather than landing where they took off. Not only was this decision unpopular with VIPs, it also threw the governor's security detail into a frenzy, as they would have to make a significant number of changes to their security plan.

To compound matters further, the day before the race, the FAA and air traffic controllers decided that all helicopter traffic needed to be rerouted 10 miles south of the airport. This meant that what would have been a five-minute flight from downtown to the track took 20 minutes. Each way.

Traffic was significantly less on Friday and Saturday than on Sunday, but when Sunday rolled around, René and her team were already tired. For whatever reason, Steve Henry's company did not give Charlie Bravo Charter's helicopters first right of refusal to land and take off from the track. Circling helicopters were in a holding pattern for as long as 45 minutes, requiring several of them to return to the airport to refuel instead of picking up passengers.

Pilots were irritable, passengers, who had been warned there would be somewhat of a wait, were furious, and COTA employees were completely unavailable to help. In fact, they avoided René's calls for nearly two months after the event, forcing her to refund some clients' fares on her own, even though COTA had failed to live up to the terms of the contract which required it to provide all the priority landings to Charlie Bravo.

René counted as a success that there were 2100 operations in three days without a single incident, not even a sprained ankle on the uneven ground where the helicopters landed at the track. But the overall customer experience was far below what she had hoped to provide.

There are times when you accomplish what seemed impossible and still, for reasons outside of your control, you fail. Even though René and her staff were flexible and responsive in meeting each challenge, Charlie Bravo Charter's reputation and profitability suffered.

Instead of looking back on the experience as time poorly spent on an endeavor that didn't provide the results she wanted, René chooses to remember she made good connections, kept people safe, and learned a lot about charter operations and helicopters. She certainly knows to ask more questions about how partners will perform their expected tasks. And today, she uses that experience in analyzing her clients' private aircraft missions from both a financial and a complexity standpoint.

Sometimes failure is inevitable, but there is always a silver lining in the cloud of dust stirred up by a big fleet of helicopters. You may just have to wait for it to settle to see the positive.

Be Willing to Reassess and Fix Broken Things

Lisa's experience with growth and failure took a different route. Fiat of Austin was the top performing dealership in the nation—and it operated in a nontraditional location. One of Lisa's keenest observations in her quest to increase sales to women is that women like to shop more than they like to buy. So she gave them a shopping experience. Fiat of Austin occupied a mere 6,000 square feet of retail space in the Domain, an upscale shopping and dining center in a growing part of North Austin. Though Tesla and others have since copied Lisa's model, it was unprecedented at the time.

The location lent itself to constant foot traffic as patrons at the local spa or the Apple store or Neiman Marcus were curious about the little cars on the corner. Inside the showroom, a red carpet led to the spot where the luckiest consumers took delivery of their new Fiats. Lisa and her team created a car *shopping* experience. She hired and conditioned her salespeople with a unique value proposition: Fiat of Austin was different. They were the anti-car dealer, a high-end boutique, just like Louis Vuitton and Tiffany's around the corner. Her team loved it, and they loved her. When she broke the sales record, the average age of her employees was 25, disproving the myth that millennials cannot be motivated. In 2013, Automotive News named Fiat of Austin number six of the top 100 best dealerships to work for in the U.S. across all automobile brands!

However, the limited retail space became more and more challenging with the increasing volume of cars sold and service for Fiats located off-site. When Fiat Chrysler Automobiles decided to bring the Alfa Romeo back to the U.S. in the same outlets as the Fiats, Lisa had a choice to make in order to carry the new line. She negotiated a deal to move from her 6,000-square-foot, eight-thousand-dollar-a-month retail space to an eight-million-dollar facility on automotive row.

She anticipated the challenges of vastly increased overhead and needing to run a profitable service center. She knew she would need to sell more used cars. The team moved to the new location in January 2014. By March, Lisa saw what she had missed in her planning. She underestimated her employees' reaction to the shift in culture and environment. She knew moving into a traditional dealership would be different; she had cut her teeth in one. But her team was unprepared.

Away from the amenities they had enjoyed at the Domain, they found themselves prospecting more and selling less. Alarmed by the apparent disengagement (and a few departures) of her previously enthusiastic employees, Lisa drafted a survey and had her employees anonymously complete it. She was horrified at the results. She divided her people into four groups and tackled the problems. She apologized profusely for letting them down and got back to the basics. She studied workplace cultures in other industries and appointed a Chief Happiness Officer to stay abreast of any arising problems. As a result, Fiat/Alfa Romeo of Austin was back on the list of top dealerships to work for in 2015. To keep succeeding after a setback, you must be willing to hear honest feedback and make adjustments.

Sometimes You Admit Failure and Take a Different Path

One of the most anticipated new baseball players of all time was a man who knew tremendous success in life and athletics, Michael Jordan. Michael left the NBA, a three-time champion and sports icon, to pursue his love of baseball and a chance to be a star in another industry. The harsh reality was this mega-star went to a minor league baseball team, rode on buses that were not nearly as comfortable as the cars he owned, and took a beating from reporters and spectators all over the country. While he was the best basketball player of his time, his talents in baseball proved subpar. He played for three different minor league teams in his attempt to get the call to the big leagues. It never came.

Michael was asked over and over, "What made you keep trying baseball after you failed?" When he returned to the NBA, two years after leaving it, Nike came out with a commercial that summed up his thoughts on what makes a winner: He said, "I've missed more than 9,000 shots in my career. I've lost almost 300 games; 26 times I've been trusted to take the game winning shot, and missed. I've failed over and over and over again in my life...and that is why I succeed."

> **Maybe we should let those younger than us fail, so they learn how to pick themselves up, brush themselves off, and run to catch up.**

Failure is a necessary part of success. It helps you remain humble. It promotes growth. You must not be afraid to look foolish or lose face. You must know when to not take failure personally. You must, like Thomas

Edison, commit to success despite setbacks. And you must know that the worst is usually not as bad as you imagined it could be.

As a society, we are doing a huge disservice to the generation behind ours, the generation that overwhelmingly wants to be difference-makers and world-changers. We have celebrated "good enough" and "great try" and told them "we're not going to let you fail" and "no child gets left behind." We have made inclusion a greater priority than excellence. The problem is, we are not teaching fortitude, drive, tenacity, or perseverance.

If we don't teach them how to crush mediocrity after failure and stand a head above the crowd, we may rob them of the legacy they otherwise could leave. And the compounding effect as generations come and go will be disastrous.

9
Use Your Influence for Good

We can rise above the status quo by
focusing on others instead of ourselves.

Ever since the genesis of motion pictures, Hollywood has banked on the knowledge that everyone loves a hero. The actor doesn't necessarily need to have tights and a cape (although it doesn't hurt). He or she just needs to overcome the obstacle and save the day. The bigger the villain, the more we cheer for the underdog.

We love our heroes on the silver screen and in real life. In fact, most of us would like to be one. Unfortunately, many of us put off the first step, thinking that we will help others when we have more time or when we have a lot more money. But if we do something with what we have today, we can make an impact right now. We can lend a hand, encourage a neighbor with a kind word, or make an introduction that will kindle new business opportunities.

As time goes on, the more money or resources we have, the better we can do. If we get in the habit of hoarding influence or being stingy, we will just propagate that negative mindset as our influence grows. Several years ago, René helped a client buy an aircraft from a well-known public figure. The seller complained even when things were going exactly as he wanted. In fact, this sports icon is notorious for not being particularly moral or generous. As the transaction was drawing to a close and the man was getting uglier in his demands, René recommended that his attorney buy him a new bed so that he could get out of it on the right side. The attorney laughed and said that he was *always* that dissatisfied. Always. He wields power for his own benefit instead of for others—and it sure seems that he finds no happiness in it.

Use What You Have

The truth of the matter is that you can choose to wield power like a weapon of mass destruction, or you can exert your influence for good. You can do it today. Right where you are now. The happiest people we know are those, regardless of wealth, who expend their resources, time, and influence on behalf of others. While American First Ladies have always extended inspiring influence, the story of Zainularab Miri in Laura Bush's *We Are Afghan Women: Voices of Hope*[26], humbled us as much as it inspired us. Zainularab found success in an environment so different from ours that we cannot even imagine it.

Her story is different than that of many Afghan women because her father allowed her to be educated alongside her brothers. She played chess when they played chess. She went to college and was certified to teach Dari, the native language of Afghanistan. Those opportunities made the oppression of the Taliban and its rules outlawing the education of females all the harder for Zainularab. Here's her story:

"Although my family was very progressive, Afghanistan is a very traditional society. Historically, men have frowned on women working outside of the home. It has been considered an affront to the man that he cannot support his wife himself or be a father who cannot support his daughters. But I wanted a profession, and for a woman, one of the best ones was teaching, so in college I studied education and child development. I got married as I started my career… But I did not just teach.

I was very lucky to have married a man who is just as open-minded as my father. As I moved around teaching, I realized that there were five men in our area of Ghazni who kept bees. In Afghanistan, bee-keeping is traditionally a male job. But that only made me more passionate to learn the business. As when I played soccer or chess as a girl, just like my brothers, I wanted to be like these men. I wanted to keep bees. I started by buying two hives from a friend of my family's, and as part of the bargain, I asked him to teach me what he knew. I, the teacher of [language], became a student of bees.

Once I had my two hives, I wanted to expand. I was paid as much money for my nectar and honey as the male beekeepers were. No one thought to segregate my honey or pay me less because I was a woman. And each year, I added more hives and more bees. The Taliban did not know. They did not know that I was working, and that every year I was determined to double my cases of bees.

Interestingly, for a beekeeper, even a woman beekeeper, the part that's the most challenging is making the queen bee. Without a good queen, the hive cannot be productive. The queen is what gives life to the hive, laying as many as fifteen hundred eggs in a peak day… In a colony, the queen is the one bee that will never leave the hive. She spends her entire life inside the honeycombs. She can never escape the walls around her, never take flight. My honeybees could spread their wings and move from flower to flower or plant to plant, drinking in the sweetness. They could come and go as they pleased. I wonder if that is part of what makes honey so sweet, if it is the taste of that feeling of freedom, of flight.

As women in Afghanistan, during those Taliban years, many of us felt like the queen bee, trapped in our own hive. The bees build their honeycombs in the darkness. We too survived by working in darkness, behind curtains, under the cover of cloth; even my beekeeper suit hid who I was. But the darkness was appropriate, because the Taliban period was a very dark time for women.

When the Taliban fell however, we found that we had our own honey. The girls who had been in seventh or eighth grade when the Taliban took hold were now in twelfth grade. Those years had not become a void in their young lives. They had continued with their education. Like the bees, they couldn't leave the hive, but when it was over, their learning was our honey, the residue of all their hard work.

Each season watching my bees leave and fly off and then return laden with sweet nectar for honey fired in me a passion to be able to move about freely. But not just for me, for as many women as I could find. I believe that in order to change a country, first you must work on the women."

Zainularab used the education and the limited resources she had to help young women rise above what little was expected, or even allowed. She did it in secret, risking her life in a time and place and regime where women's lives didn't count for much. May we all be so brave.

Use Situational Awareness

One of the most critical skills in aviation, and in life, is situational awareness. Wikipedia defines it as "the perception of environmental elements with respect to time or space, the comprehension of their meaning, and the projection of their status after some variable has changed... Situation awareness involves being aware of what is happening in the vicinity to understand how information, events, and one's actions will impact goals and objectives, both immediately and in the near future."[27]

In piloting an airplane, for instance, you have to look at the meteorological environment, your instruments, and your surroundings. Almost all "user error" diagnoses stem from a lack of situational awareness. You have to know the resources you have—even if they are small—and use them.

The car business lends itself to awareness of community needs because it touches people on a daily basis. Car dealers, especially the more prosperous ones, seem to have an unspoken competition to outdo each other in giving back.

Randall Reed began his career as an auto mechanic, but that wasn't enough for him. He focused on being the best mechanic in his shop. After a while, he was elevated to manager and eventually became the owner of a dealership. As his wealth grew, so did his influence.

Today, Randall owns eight dealerships across several states. He makes it a point to give in the communities where his dealerships are, and not just with tax dollars and local jobs, which is common with all dealerships. Randall looks for people who need help and the organizations that are equipped to provide that assistance directly.

Several years ago, Randall realized that there was an application that would help autistic children with speech impediments to communicate with their teachers and caretakers by selecting icons on a touch screen. He bought six iPads with the application installed for the local school district and changed what was possible for many students and their families. One young woman named Courtney, who was wheelchair-bound with Cerebral Palsy, was so grateful that through the interface she asked her hero (Randall) if he would dance with her at the Village Learning Center's annual gala.

Kristi Williams, who handles community relations at his Humble, Texas Ford dealership took Courtney shopping for a dress and arranged to have her hair and makeup done. The night of the dance Randall sent a limo to pick her up, and they danced. It was one of the most special nights of her short life, according to her mom, and she was thrilled to have the ability to communicate her feelings. Courtney died just two months later of complications of an intestinal rupture, one she couldn't feel because of her paralysis. Without Randall's iPad and application donation, Courtney's family would never have had meaningful conversations with her.

Randall believes that teachers are the heart of the community, as they both educate and help mold the lives of our future leaders. He and his staff also believe that teachers are under-recognized and under-compensated for the important work they do. Several years ago, Randall and his teams decided to begin donating a new car to the Teacher of the Year in several school districts they serve. They select one teacher from each school and then narrow down the finalists to award a car and a cruise to the top two teachers respectively. The program has been wildly successful, making recruiting teachers more competitive and improving job satisfaction overall across the districts.

With the popularity and proven results of the programs Randall supports, he has been able to use his influence to get other business leaders involved in their respective communities. Some of the charities he supports have been able to help more people—veterans, single moms, and children—through exponentially increased fundraising. Randall puts money, time, and other resources to work to positively impact the world around him.

Josh "Chop" Towbin, who starred in an American Reality show, *King of Cars* on the A&E television network, also owns a number of car dealerships, some of the most active in the country. Unlike Randall, Chop was born into the automotive trade, but with a stubborn streak, he was determined to make it on his own without help from his dad.

He started work as a porter in the dealership washing cars at a young age. He sold mopeds and scooters on the side. By age 15, Chop bought and sold cars for cash. And at 16, he had worked his way up to manager of the lot porter staff and then moved to the sales floor. It didn't take long for him to become the top salesperson and then the used car sales manager. By the time he was 22, Chop was running Towbin Dodge, where he continues breaking sales records today—now as an owner.

Chop has taken a chance on hundreds of employees who just needed someone to believe in them and encourage them, even if they didn't look like the typical sales person. Along with several of his managers, Chop mentors young adults who have aged-out of the foster care program in Nevada, working through St. Jude's Ranch and other programs. These young adults regularly come into the dealership to see the kinds of careers they can build in the automotive industry. And if they aren't interested in cars, the information Chop teaches also helps them know how to interview, negotiate pay, choose the right career, and stay employed after being hired.

When we visited his dealership recently, we were able to witness a fun interview process in which applicants audition for sales jobs in an American Idol-type format. Chop believes it builds the culture of the organization when co-workers have the opportunity to be both vulnerable and encouraging.

This philosophy about caring for others, especially those who might not have anyone else in their corner, helps Towbin's dealerships sell a lot of cars—and provide a great living for those fortunate enough to work there.

And, yes, Chop gives away his fair share of cars also, but you don't need a lot of money or the ability to give away cars to use your influence for good. You just need the heart to help.

Follow Your Passions

Cherie Mathews puts her hand to work where her heart is. Cherie is a former IBM research and development computer engineer and inventor who was diagnosed at 40 with breast cancer. She had to have a double mastectomy. In addition to the emotional and physical trauma of going home without the "girls," Cherie was shocked at her treatment in the hospital. She had difficulty getting dressed with what she brought to go home in, her husband's dress shirt, which was suggested by her doctor.

As she was struggling to put on a men's button down shirt, she asked the nurse for assistance. The nurse appeared annoyed that Cherie needed her help and, with a deep exhale, handed her two safety pins to attach the surgical drains to the outside of the shirt. Perplexed, Cherie said, "This is my first mastectomy. I'm not sure of the protocol here, but why doesn't the hospital provide something easier for women to go home in?"

Cherie huffed all the way home about a sprained elbow or ankle getting better-suited equipment than a surgery as traumatic as a mastectomy. She didn't like the nurse's response that women had always just suffered the indignity in silence. Cherie decided to do something about it. Cancer had picked on the wrong girl.

To start, Cherie designed and patented a post-operative shirt with "soft as feathers" moisture management material, Velcro-like fasteners for independent dressing and four internal pockets to discreetly conceal the surgical drains. "Women can now be discharged from the hospital looking like a person and not a science experiment," she said. "Cancer is hard enough and this post-operative garment is one thing off the never-ending list of concerns while battling this horrible disease."

Cherie's proof of concept goal was 100 patients. That has turned into 10,000, and her product has won many local and national awards for innovation. Cherie's end goal is to change the discharge procedure for mastectomy patients so every woman will be provided a healincomfort™ recovery shirt to go home in and begin the healing process.

Cherie used her experience with breast cancer and her innovative abilities to create a solution to restore dignity to women. She now mass produces the shirts and ships them globally. She also helped set up a non-profit to provide shirts in her hometown and hardship cases throughout the U.S. If you know someone who can benefit from Cherie's experiences, the online store can be found at www.healincomfort.com, and the 501(c)3 that is independently run by volunteers is GiftingCare.org.

Tony Selvaggio lives in Tampa, Florida, a far cry from his poverty-stricken birth country Venezuela. As his situation in life improved, Tony sought ways to help others—both in Venezuela and in his adopted country. Even though he had a meager bank account, Tony took action. He began to collect old computers people no longer used and refurbish them. He gave them away to needy schools and financially challenged organizations.

As Tony's work gained attention, other people joined the cause and began introducing him to people who could help, such as IT managers at large companies. Soon after, his company, eSmart Recycling, was born. Now, because of the donations of companies and other patrons, Tony has been able to donate an entire tech lab to one of the poorer schools in Venezuela and has helped underprivileged students in Tampa have the same resources as others.

Tony proves that generosity doesn't always come from wealth but from a commitment to do good for others. Like Cherie and Tony, you can take something that stirs your passions and turn it into something positive for those around you. You have more than you think.

Connect the Dots

Robin Eissler has been around aviation all her life. She flew a plane solo before she drove a car. She took a field trip in college to help a pilot deliver a King Air to South Africa from the U.S.—33 hours of flying with landings in some pretty crazy places like Iceland and Senegal. Robin's dad and brother are in the aviation business with her. Her husband Trevor flies planes for a large aircraft fractional ownership program. She knows firsthand how nimble and helpful small planes can be.

Robin and Trevor lived in Boca Raton when their twins were born prematurely in 2004, which is known as the Year of Four Hurricanes in Florida. They were evacuated while their babies were in the neonatal intensive care unit (NICU) at their local hospital. Their twins remained in the wake of the hurricane while Robin and Trevor were hundreds of miles away. The stress this caused for Robin was one of the biggest contributors for the family's move away from the coastline to central Texas.

In the days following Hurricane Katrina's devastation of New Orleans in 2006, Robin watched the news and relived the trauma of being separated from loved ones. She saw a segment about babies being airlifted from hospitals. She was determination to help, even if she had to pay to use her company's airplane.

Robin said, "After numerous calls to news stations and hospitals, I finally found a woman at a central command center at Houston Children's Hospital who understood the value of what we were offering and she said she would find a mission for us. I posted an e-mail on a private aircraft forum to see if anyone else wanted to help. By the next morning, I had more than a dozen responses from individuals and corporations willing to donate their aircraft to do whatever was necessary."

Two days went by with no calls. Things became worse in New Orleans and Mississippi. More families were being separated. Robin made more phone calls, this time to the Red Cross, both local and national, to other hospitals, and to the air ambulance company coordinating the relief effort. Still, no takers. "It was like having all the pieces to play chess, but no board to play on," she said.

Finally, one of her friends had a breakthrough. She found a Christian disaster relief organization with contacts in Baton Rouge who could coordinate efforts there. They knew of several churches that were housing evacuees and were nearly out of food, water and diapers. Robin coordinated efforts with suppliers, planes, and on-location relief groups to get supplies around flooded roads and into desperate areas. Within a few weeks, with a team of impromptu volunteers, she was coordinating 15 to 30 flights a day, delivering supplies and reuniting families.

Little did Robin know, her response to Hurricane Katrina was just on-the-job-training for what was to come. On January 12, 2010, when Haiti was rocked by a catastrophic earthquake, Robin didn't waste time calling the Red Cross. She didn't wait to see how bad the devastation was. She knew smaller planes that require shorter runway length and less clearance would be able to land in Haiti before commercial airline service resumed. She wanted to be ready as soon as the aftershocks stopped. She reestablished the channels she used during Hurricane Katrina.

Within hours, Robin had details on all the airstrips (paved or unpaved) that could support private planes, from pilots who had landed on them in the past. She had dozens of aircraft on alert and dozens of Non-Government Organizations (NGOs) assembling supplies and volunteers ready to go on a few hours' notice. As a result, Sky Hope Network, which is what Robin later named the organization she was forming on the fly, flew 60 missions in and out of Haiti before the Red Cross had their first team on the ground!

The silver lining in the cloud was that as a poverty-stricken area, there were already a number of charitable organizations on the ground in a position to distribute food, medical supplies, and other necessary items. Over a five-month period, Robin and a massive team of make-something-happen volunteers organized more than 900 flights that moved more than 2,000,000 pounds of supplies and 1,200 medical personnel—and directly saved the lives of more than a dozen individuals.

Our favorite story among all of those about lives saved, patients treated, destitute people fed, and families reunited originated with a call to Robin's cell phone. The head of Notre Dame's nursing school in Leogane, Haiti, requested support from the airlift. Without any electricity at all, he feared patients would begin dying. All roads to the remote area were cut off, and supplies could not come in by boat. The only hope was Robin's ability to get a small plane to the area. The locals mentioned a drug runner had once landed on a road in the town.

Robin had a Caravan pilot do a fly over. He said it was possible if they cut a few trees away. And then he began his missions, five to six a day, flying in supplies, allowing fuel to be siphoned out of his tank to power the generators, and moving critically ill patients to hospitals in better-supplied areas.

Find Your Style

Like Robin and these other examples, people who change their piece of the world tend to do well by doing good. They see a bigger picture, look for time or resource investment opportunities, make connections, rally the troops, and take action.

As we've illustrated through these amazing stories, there are many ways to wield influence. Moreover, when there is a real need, and you're in a funk and don't feel like helping, that's exactly the right time to focus on others instead of yourself. That's what heroes do! You just have to find a style that fits you.

Lisa's style is very inclusive. Once she rallies behind a cause, she invites everyone she knows to get involved. Nobody's checkbook or contact list is sacred. A great example is the number of women she persuaded to join the Girl Scouts initiative to fund STEM learning, obtaining $3000 commitments from more than 100 women in her sphere of influence and securing a $250,000 grant by pulling strings in the automotive industry.

René tends to offer financial support quietly to organizations she knows are making a difference in people's lives. One example is a fishing ministry that delivers thousands of pounds of fresh fish a year to feed the kids in Los Cabos, Mexico barrios. Another is an anti-trafficking organization that rescued a number of young women in Romania who had been enclosed in a wall as prisoners.

One of the organizations we support together gives hundreds of $300 micro-loans to women in India so they can start their own businesses. These women do much with very little, and they are a great example of crushing mediocrity for their families and communities.

In her foreword for **We Are Afghan Women**, Laura Bush states: "Women reinvest 90 percent of their income in three key areas: educating their children, accessing health care for their family, and growing their local economy."[28] Each day, you choose how you're going to use your time, your talents, your connections, your education, your resources, and your influence. How are you going to use it for good?

10
Become a Change Agent

*If we create a positive culture shift,
we crush mediocrity at its roots.*

Our great-grandparents witnessed massive advancements over their lifetimes. They drove some of the first gasoline-powered automobiles. They were among the first women to vote in the United States. They were the first generation with telephones, electricity, radios, televisions, dishwashers, microwaves, and vacuum cleaners in their homes. They were alive during the first powered flight and the first man on the moon—and all this innovation happened despite the disruption of two world wars and the Great Depression.

We came of age as the Internet was first emerging. We were the first users of personal computers, Memorex tapes, email, and mobile phones. In fact, we were the first users of cordless phones, car phones, brick phones, cell phones, iPhones, and whatever else has come out by the time this book lands in your hands. The pace of change is increasing rapidly.

Several scientific formulas suggest we will advance roughly the same amount in the next 18 months as we did in the previous 30 years. [29]

In aviation, we are closely watching the development of passenger drones, self-flying vehicles that will radically change how we manage airspace and travel. Innovative companies in retail sales are anticipating great changes as well, one of which will be virtual sales people at kiosks. We call these major advances a disrupter. Dictionary.com indicates to disrupt is to "change radically (for example, an industry or business strategy) by introducing a new product or service that creates a new market."

Disrupters can be good. They can also be bad. Families are disrupted by divorce. Lives are hijacked by terrorism or disease. Cars crash. Pets die. People make mistakes. You have to decide how you're going to handle the disruptions in your life or sphere of influence, and know that each one may require a different approach.

React Wisely

Our friend Amy Dillon got hit with three major disrupters in a very short period. Amy was happily married with a small child, a flourishing women's ministry, and a passion for running when she started having back pains. The doctor recommended surgery to remove the tumor buried deep in her spinal cord.

When the doctor came out of surgery, he looked frazzled, and those of us in the waiting room were worried. He said the tumor was so far-reaching that it looked like a grenade had gone off inside her spine and that she would never run again. In fact, he wasn't certain she would even walk again. While the tumor was benign, the damage it had inflicted was irreparable.

Amy refused to believe the prognosis, that this was her fate. She challenged his report and after 30 days she took her first steps. After six months, she no longer used a wheelchair. And three years, two months, and sixteen days after that dreadful report, she wore high-heeled wedges. She still dreams of running again.

With her life radically altered by immobility, Amy struggled to find the energy to prepare speeches and stand in front of crowds. It took everything she had to hold her family together. She lost her ministry, her purpose, and her drive. To make matters worse, just as she was beginning to stand on her own two feet, figuratively and literally, her husband left her for another woman. Applying the same tenacity that she used to walk again, she fought valiantly for her marriage. It didn't work. She couldn't power through. He pressured her to sign the divorce papers. Then he remarried. She began to pick up the pieces.

Today, as a thriving sales executive, Amy is rebuilding her speaking platform. She says letting go of her ministry dreams helped them to mature in a way she could never have anticipated. Fighting to

Someone has to show my daughter that although life can get you down, you have to get back up.
-*Amy Dillon*

walk again, hour after painful hour, gave her focus and determination. And losing her husband, well, that honed her faith and introspection to the point that she knows exactly who she is and where she is headed.

Amy turned three different results from three different types of disrupters into something she can be proud of going into the future. She has since purchased a home and is earning a great income to provide for herself and her daughter. Now she is a disrupter herself, a shining light for women in despair, offering encouragement to those on the brink of giving up. By not letting potentially catastrophic personal and physical events alter who she is, Amy Dillon has the ability and the credibility to encourage us all.

Several years ago, René's escrow agent, Debbie Mercer-Erwin, lived through a parent's worst nightmare. She had spent a quiet evening with her 22-year-old son Kyle, who told her he wasn't feeling well before he went to his sister Kayleigh's house for one last night of house sitting. Early the next day, Debbie picked up Kayleigh at the airport and dropped her off at home. Several minutes later, Kayleigh found Kyle lying on the bed, one leg hanging off, with his shoe untied. He was dead. She called 911 and then called her mom, frantic.

Despite her son dying inexplicably, Debbie did not drop a single detail of an aircraft closing that week. She grieved. She still grieves sometimes. But keeping an eye on her business kept her from losing her mind, she says. It wasn't until six weeks after the funeral, his autopsy revealed Kyle died from a serious lung infection, a complication of pneumonia. He hadn't taken his antibiotics prescription.

When major disrupters threaten your sanity, hanging on to the stable things can keep you from spinning out of control. Six months after Kyle died, Debbie had the opportunity to help a friend whose son died from a fatal drug overdose. While her friend is still struggling today, Debbie's focus on work, family, and building her legacy helped her through the difficult time. In our book, that's rising above the status quo!

Be Encouraging

Changing our world does no broad-reaching good if we are not doing it for a lasting effect. As parents and teachers, coaches and managers, presidents and five-year-old-organizers-of-kindergarten-games-of-tag, we must take steps to help make those around us better. To be a true agent of change requires us to come out of our comfort zone and mentor someone, even if they belong to a generation we don't understand. It forces us to confront bullies. It makes us get involved in people's real lives, regardless of how messy, instead of watching "reality" on exaggerated, over-produced television shows. It encourages us to tell the truth instead of copping out with a "politically correct" answer. It holds others—and ourselves—to a higher standard.

In short, if you are going to disrupt the status quo, you must be willing to learn from others around you and invest in them. You have to risk being hurt or disappointed. You must work hard to answer generational challenges, such as understanding the appeal of pooled resources or appreciating the work ethic in a nine-to-five job.

Don't fall into the trap of a mediocre mindset, instead, be a person who hasn't given up on the next generation or a person that views the older generation as relevant and full of wisdom. Be a person who strives for meaningful friendships with people of all ages and who respects their opinions instead of trying to control them. It takes people with compassion and tenacity to change the lives of others. You can do it—and it doesn't always take a great deal of effort.

Not one of us can change the whole world by ourselves. As we have stated throughout this book, we each need to do our part. We must be purposeful, and we need to rely on and encourage one another. We must be prepared to rise above the status quo every chance we get. Sometimes the chances we take work. Sometimes they won't. But without taking chances on others, we cannot help them.

One man took that opportunity in René's life. Howard Hollinger had nothing to gain by calling René to congratulate her on an *Austin American Statesman* article about her business. He merely felt a kinship because he also had attended Ohio University, and the article mentioned that. Once he knew her story, he began hounding the alumni magazine at OU to write an article as well. Several years went by. Howard, who was in failing health, kept in touch. He also kept reminding the OU alumni association about René, until they wrote the article.

When Curt and René met with the director of alumni relations, Curt asked what René would need to do to finish the degree she was forced to abandon when she got pregnant. Encouraged by their interest, the director invited René to speak at a Global Women in Entrepreneurship Day event at the university. The request came just days after Lisa and René landed on the title for this book, and René used the opportunity to test her thoughts about crushing mediocrity. University leaders used the visit to define René's graduation requirements. It would be 20 hours of projects and classes, the maximum allowed per semester.

While still working full-time at Charlie Bravo Aviation, René once again became a full-time student, cramming in all of the 20 remaining hours to get her degree. She also took time to visit Howard and his wife Rose and shared the video of the speech she gave. Howard beamed. Rose grasped his hand and smiled. Her "Holly," as she called him, was always encouraging others, she said. He noticed people. He believed the best of them. And he had changed countless lives over their 60 years of marriage.

He passed from this life just a few days after René visited, so Howard Hollinger will never know the impact he made in the writing of this book. His encouragement sparked a journey that resulted in this material in your hands right now. What you do with it is up to you. Maybe it will help someone else to do something great with just a few words of encouragement from you.

Listen

Perhaps even more important than "speaking" positive things into people's lives is listening. Anatomy tells us we should spend twice as much time listening as talking;

that's the reason we have one mouth and two ears. Our challenge is to filter out the noise and really listen to what others say, especially those whose opinions, actions, and expectations impact the world around us.

Richard Branson attributes some of Virgin's success to good communication skills. "Listen – it makes you sound smarter," he says. We love that! When we attentively listen to what others have to say, it gives us a competitive edge we wouldn't otherwise have.

NY Times Bestselling Authors Adrian Gostick and Chester Elton talk with companies all over the world about building positive cultures. Listening is a key element. Here's what they said when we asked what they had learned:

"For a leader, it's always nice to hear positive feedback from our employees. 'Boss, things are going well, your ideas are being implemented, and your strategy seems right on track.' Unfortunately, none of us lives in a Disney movie. Often our concepts could use some improvement; our direction might be flawed, or perhaps we've taken our eyes off our customers' needs. To create a true partnership, we need our employees to know we are listening—and we need to know when something isn't working. Too many leaders aren't willing to really listen to negative feedback from their people.

Furthermore, it's clear that if more companies listened to their customers, fewer would face ignominious ends. Too many of us are oblivious to what customers find attractive about our rivals; we live in a self-reverential bliss. It's a decades-old trend. Many of the world's top companies from the mid-1980s have foundered, shrunk, grown obsolete, or been acquired by rivals that grew stronger. Digital Equipment and Wang Laboratories, once leading computer firms, disappeared completely. Even titans like Apple and IBM once stared into the abyss of irrelevance and had to make painful changes before clawing their way back to the top.

One of the reasons for this aversion to listening to customer trends and feedback is the fundamental human tendency to filter out information that does not match up with our preconceived notions. We call this *confirmation bias*. This leads many of us to genuinely think that our products or services are superior when we should be open-minded about our limitations. One of the most effective ways of overcoming this bias, is to create a culture of rigorous customer focus with channels for all employees (especially frontline sales) to report upward issues that they are seeing while working with clients. In fact, the most profitable cultures we have studied not only listen for customer feedback but can be described as *active* in soliciting both the good and the bad—and consider seriously even some comments or criticisms that may seem off-the-wall at the time. As we're sure you have witnessed, in most companies, negative customer feedback is hidden from view; feedback that could lead to new directions all too often is ignored."[30]

What you don't know can and will hurt you. So, don't just listen, pay attention.

Be Relevant

If we are going to disrupt the status quo in the world around us, we must be relevant. We have to get involved and know what's important in other people's lives. With the overload of information making unprecedented noise and people trying to be all things to all people, authenticity still rings loud and clear.

Susan Scarola was the Special Projects Manager at DCH Auto Group for years before she became the CFO. She had become the trusted go-to-girl when the management team needed something done right. The year was 2007. DCH Auto Group had 40 dealerships, each running fairly independently with their own set of values and operations, and Susan was set to retire in a few months. What she didn't know was that turmoil was about to hit the industry, and hard.

Instead of accepting Susan's retirement, the owners of DCH requested that she accept the position of CEO and undertake the task of uniting the brand and corporate culture, a monumental task even in the best of times. She agreed to a four-year contract and made a plan to change the corporate culture radically to one of transparency, integrity, and respect in the dealerships spread across the country. Her story of tenacity in the face of skepticism, discrimination, and financial doom is a great tale of rising above the status quo.

Susan took heat in the press when she fired key employees in the middle of the recession. She walked through every corner of each dealership and rooted out inadequacies and less-than-stellar practices. Susan shook hands with every worker and knew about their struggles and strengths. She overruled managers who didn't want their employees interacting with potential clients on social media, forcing relevancy in a changing digital marketplace. She started a teen safe-driving program to give back to the communities in every market DCH served, and built a foundation to support the work. It was a daunting task to overhaul the methodologies and ingrained practices of such a large organization, but she didn't look at it as if she was fixing a company. In her mind, she was building a legacy. Overcoming the odds, she succeeded in changing the culture and positioning DCH as a very attractive acquisition prospect. She was relevant.

Stay Focused on the Good

We have been blessed to meet many amazing people in business and our communities. We've introduced you to a few of them in the pages of this book. However, our last story is the best example of rising above circumstances to pull something good out of something bad.

John and Erin Kiltz, and their children Emily and Riley, were the quintessential American family when baby Grace was born with Down Syndrome. Regardless of her disability, Grace's smile could light up a Texas sky, and she developed as normally as a little girl could. Then, at age two, Grace was diagnosed with a rare and aggressive form of leukemia. The family visited the hospital regularly during Grace's full year of inpatient chemotherapy treatments.

Grace showed signs of rallying; however, when she was three she developed a triple bacterial infection and was rushed to the emergency department. The triage nurses failed to communicate with each other, and four hours went by without anyone checking Gracie's blood pressure. That simple test would have shown she was septic. Instead, the sepsis ran rampant in her little body and resulted in a 20-minute flat line. The lack of oxygen to her brain and other organs left Grace blind and in a vegetative state. It left her parents nearly hopeless.

They were told that Grace, their little sunshine, would never recognize them again, would not be able to eat, and would never walk or be able to communicate. Worst of all, the part of her brain that controlled her smile was completely obliterated. As John and Erin were struggling with their next steps, Emily, seven, and Riley, five, would climb into Grace's crib, sing to her, and pray that her smile would come back. And then, six months later, it did.

Instead of suing the hospital for millions of dollars, as their lawyers and friends recommended, Erin started a foundation to bring hope to other families spending weeks or months or years walking the hallways while their children suffered. The Grace Foundation is still active nearly 20 years later. Grace learned to chew. She began recognizing friends and family members. She even attended the same high school as her sister and brother. Over the years, her smile has only become more infectious.

In fact, in October 2010, the students at Georgetown High School, a large public school in an Austin suburb, nominated and then elected Grace and another special needs student, Jared Friemel, Homecoming Queen and King. That little girl, who wasn't expected to be any more than an unresponsive vegetable made national news.

Right after Homecoming, Erin began exploring the choices for Grace's years after graduation. The options were dismal. She searched every program in the state and finally found one she thought she could replicate. And she's had unprecedented support from the community.

Today Brookwood in Georgetown, or BiG, gives hope to its "citizens" and their caretakers. BiG is an entrepreneurial vocational community where adults (including Grace) with intellectual challenges are celebrated and empowered by engaging their talents in meaningful work. The citizens make handmade pottery pieces that sit on the shelves at the local Whole Foods. Their greeting cards grace thousands of mailboxes. The café they run usually has a line. And the sunflowers they grow exude happiness.

Photos of sunflowers coupled with inspirational quotes line the walls at BiG. Erin explains: "Sunflowers have seeds that can lie dormant for years. Given the opportunity and the right conditions to grow, these seeds are activated and bloom into breathtaking flowers. BiG citizens are like these seeds. Our nurturing environment may be the factor, like sunlight on dormant seeds, helping them blossom into their full potential."

We believe that every person can rise above the status quo. If Gracie Kiltz, the Down Syndrome and leukemia sufferer who developed a triple bacterial infection, can become Homecoming Queen and live a rich life, so can you. If you were to take another look at what's blocking your path to crushing mediocrity and compare it to what Gracie has been through, you'd see what we see: There is no reason you can't become an agent for change. None.

Conclusion

It's easy to identify what's wrong with your family, your workplace, and your community. It's trying to change what's wrong that requires strategy and determination. But you know it's a battle worth waging. You must not be afraid to own your choices, be humble, recover from failure, stand out, repurpose your fears, use your influence for good, and work together with others. No matter your age, the generation behind yours is starving for authenticity and role models. You must be ready with meaningful answers that are well thought out and real-life tested.

We applaud you for taking the time to read this book. We interviewed our friends and many of the other leaders in this book to highlight different ways people rise above the status quo. We didn't put pen to paper to talk about ourselves or other people we know or admire. We did it to start a revolution, to bring about change with a few dozen or a few million other people who also want to *live* a legacy and leave the world a better place, people who want to crush mediocrity and rise above the status quo.

We know your story is or will be as dynamic and life-changing as the ones we've told in these pages. We want to hear about it, believe with you, celebrate your victories, encourage you, and equip you in whatever way we can. We want to empower people to live out what the 19th-century poet Matthew Arnold described when he said, "If there ever comes a time when the women of the world come together purely and simply for the benefit of mankind, it will be a force such as the world has never known."[31]

We urge you to take the next step.

At www.crushingitacademy.com you can connect with us and with other like-minded people who no longer want to stay stuck in the status quo. We have dynamic resources, stories, practical advice, and information on how to do the things we've discussed in this book. Being part of this community may well be what you've been searching for.

We hope to see you on Crushing It Academy!

Endnotes

Chapter 1
Identify Your Purpose

1. "Having a Sense of Purpose May Add Years to Your Life," *Association for Psychological Science* (2014). Accessed July 21, 2016. http://www.psychologicalscience.org/index.php/news/releases/having-a-sense-of-purpose-in-life-may-add-years-to-your-life.html

2. Neighmond, Patti. "People Who Feel They Have a Purpose in Life Live Longer," *NPR* (2014). Accessed July 21, 2016. http://www.npr.org/sections/health-shots/2014/07/28/334447274/people-who-feel-they-have-a-purpose-in-life-live-longer

3. Sinek, Simon. "How Great Leaders Inspire Action," *TED* (2009). Accessed July 21, 2016.https://www.ted.com/talks/simon_sinek_how_great_leaders_inspire_action?language=en#t-2382

4. Sinek, Simon, *Start With Why: How Great Leaders Inspire Everyone to Take Action*. Portfolio; Reprint Edition, December 2011.

5. Warren, Rick. *The Purpose Driven Life: What on Earth Am I Here For?* Zondervan, Expanded Edition, 2013.

Chapter 2
Exit Your Comfort Zone

6. *Dictionary.com Unabridged.* "Character." Random House, Inc. Accessed July 21, 2016. http://www.dictionary.com/browse/character

7. CITRS. "What is Character?" Accessed July 21, 2016. http://www.citrs.org/what-is-character/

8. Brooks, David. *The Road to Character.* Random House, 2015.

Chapter 3
Own Your Choices

9. Hyatt, Michael. "5 Days to Your Best Year Ever." Online class (2015). http://bestyearever.me/

10. Smedes, Lewis B. *Forgive and Forget: Healing the Hurts We Don't Deserve.* HarperOne, 1984.

Chapter 4
Remain Teachable

11. Eastman, P.D. *Are You My Mother?* Random House, 1960.

12. Sandberg, Sheryl. *Lean In: Women, Work, and the Will to Lead.* Knopf, 2013

Chapter 5
Operate Together

13. Bob Seger & the Silver Bullet Band, "Against the Wind," Capital Records, 1980.

14. *Goodreads.com.* "Arnold, Matthew." Accessed July 21, 2016. http://www.goodreads.com/quotes/413325-if-there-ever-comes-a-time-when-the-women-of

15. *Urban Dictionary.* "Hater." Accessed July 21, 2016. http://www.urbandictionary.com/define.php?term=hater&utm_source=search-action

16. *Zootopia*, directed by Byron Howard, Rich Moore and Jared Bush, Walt Disney Animation Studios, 2016.

17. *I Love Lucy*, Season 2, Episode 1, September 15, 1952

Chapter 6
Stand Out

18. Time Magazine, "100 Most Important People of the 20th Century," 1999
19. Brand Finance, "Lego Overtakes Ferrari as the World's Most Powerful Brand," accessed July 21, 2016. http://brandfinance.com/news/press-releases/lego-overtakes-ferrari-as-the-worlds-most-powerful-brand/

Chapter 7
Repurpose Your Fears

20. Wikipedia, "Fight of Flight Response," accessed July 21, 2016 https://en.wikipedia.org/wiki/Fight-or-flight_response

21. Dr. Spencer Johnson, *Who Moved My Cheese?: An Amazing Way to Deal with Change in Your Work and in Your Life*. G.P Putnam's Sons, 1998.

Chapter 8
Recover From Failure

22. Pew Research Center, "The Global Religious Landscape," December 18, 2012, accessed on July 21, 2016. http://www.pewforum.org/2012/12/18/global-religious-landscape-exec/

23. Wikipedia, "Walt Disney," accessed on July 21, 2016. en.wikipedia.org/wiki/Walt_Disney

24. Wikipedia, "Colonel Sanders," accessed on July 21, 2016. en.wikipedia.org/wiki/Colonel_Sanders

25. Wikipedia, "Oprah Winfrey," accessed on July 21, 2016. https://en.wikipedia.org/wiki/Oprah_Winfrey

Chapter 9
Use Your Influence For Good

26. George W. Bush Institute, *We Are Afghan Women: Voices of Hope*. Scribner 2016.

27. Wikipedia, "Situation Awareness," accessed on July 21, 2016. https://en.wikipedia.org/wiki/Situation_awareness

28. Laura Bush, foreword to *We Are Afghan Women: Voices of Hope*, by George W. Bush Institute. Scribner 2016.

Chapter 10
Become a Change Agent

29. Greg Satell, "What Can We Expect From The Next Decade of Technology?" *Digital Tonto*, July 7, 2013, accessed July 21, 2016. http://www.digitaltonto.com/2013/what-can-we-expect-from-the-next-decade-of-technology/

30. Adrian Gostick, email message to René Banglesdorf, May 10, 2016

Conclusion

31. *Goodreads.com*. "Arnold, Matthew." Accessed July 21, 2016. http://www.goodreads.com/quotes/413325-if-there-ever-comes-a-time-when-the-women-of